AF326513

HIGH SELF-ESTEEM & CONFIDENCE MASTERY: INNER PEACE & SELF-ACCEPTANCE

*Powerful Affirmations & Hypnosis
to Increase Confidence, Self-Awareness,
Self-Worth & Self-Love for Men & Women
to Change Your Life*

Andrew Walker

that the author is not engaging in the rendering of legal, financial, medical or professional advice. The content within this book has been derived from various sources. Please consult a licensed professional before attempting any techniques outlined in this book.

By reading this document, the reader agrees that under no circumstances is the author responsible for any losses, direct or indirect, which are incurred as a result of the use of the information contained within this document, including, but not limited to, — errors, omissions, or inaccuracies.

Table of Contents

Introduction

Isn't it interesting that we so readily accept negative feedback as something true about ourselves? We are also quick to dismiss any positive feedback we hear. We easily incorporate the negative criticism into the stories we tell ourselves *about ourselves,* and we conveniently leave out the positive. This dramatically affects our lives in the present moment, it affects how our future will play out, and it affects how we view the successes and failures we will most certainly experience in life. Everyone fails, but do you believe you are destined to fail? Do you find yourself thinking things like, "I'm such a loser" or "I knew this wouldn't work out, nothing ever works out for me?" If you do, you're not alone. And this constant barrage of negative self-talk has a strong effect on your life.

If you are one of the over 300 million people worldwide who suffer from anxiety, depression, low self-esteem, low confidence, insecurity, self-doubt or a feeling of hopelessness (WHO. int, 2019), you have likely adopted negative beliefs about yourself, and you probably experience negative self-talk on a regular basis. But, the very fact that you are even thinking about reading this book means you are ready to take the necessary steps to free yourself from these damaging types of thoughts. Furthermore, you should congratulate yourself for taking this positive and often challenging first step. So, let me explain how this book can help you break the negative feedback cycle that prevents you from realizing your full potential.

One of the first questions we have to ask is where these negative beliefs come from. We often adopt beliefs about ourselves early in life. Traumas suffered during childhood are a massive source of these negative self-judgments, but it isn't always the case that it comes from traumatic or abusive events. Negative self-judgments can result from something as simple as a flippant comment from a parent or other trusted adult. It might not even be something meant to be negative, but in a child's mind, it can be turned into something quite caustic. Take for example the comment, "Practice makes perfect." It is meant to encourage a child to keep trying. The only problem is that it's often not true. If, for example, you're 5'3" tall, you're very unlikely to be the next Michael Jordan, no matter how much you practice at basketball. And when a child begins to see that the practice isn't helping, it can damage their confidence. It's easy for them to turn that into, "I'm not good enough."

On the other hand, maybe nobody ever told you anything negative, but they just didn't tell you anything positive either. Without positive support and encouragement, it is easy for the little child you were to decide you aren't good or you aren't worthy. That belief will stay buried deep inside of you, insidiously affecting your life, until you expose it for the falsehood it is.

Adopting these kinds of negative beliefs as part of your identity can dramatically alter your life. It can affect your ability to succeed in whatever type of work you pursue, it can sabotage your personal relationships, and it can lead to self-destructive behaviors such as substance abuse. The consequences of adopting these beliefs can be crippling. There is, however, something you can do to free yourself from this kind of thinking, and the purpose of this book is to show you how to do just that.

In the chapters that follow, we'll examine the difference between self-esteem and confidence, and why both are crucial to a healthy self-image. We'll then look at why powerful and positive affirmations are critical to the image you have of yourself. We'll discuss how to develop powerful affirmations and use them to view your life through a different lens, one that is healthy and supportive.

I know you may be thinking that positive affirmations are corny, and they are the butt of many jokes, but the reality is they work. Empirical evidence gathered from numerous scientific studies have shown that they reduce stress--which is a massive threat to your health, they encourage more physical activity, they are linked to positive academic achievement, and much more. Neuroscientific research (Critcher and Dunning 2015) has shown that the use of positive affirmations can increase the neural pathways in the area of our brain related to self-valuation! That means that positive affirmations help to make us more resilient when difficult situations arise in our lives because we're better able to view and utilize what might otherwise be considered self-threatening information. The bottom line is they work, but you have to practice them regularly. They have to become a habit.

After understanding how to create and practice powerful, positive affirmations, you also have to be able to reflect on who you really are, and you have to be able to accept yourself as you are, warts and all. We all are complex beings, and the reasons behind why we act in the ways we do are complicated. Understanding that will create the space in which you can truly and unconditionally accept yourself. To do that, you must also learn how to forgive yourself. It is crucial that you realize those actions are not representative of who you truly are. These tools of self-acceptance, self-reflection, and self-affirmation will help you to begin your healing process. We'll also discuss how these tools can help you to be aware of how you speak to yourself and others (and the impact that has), and how you can then build, and maintain, a strong, positive feeling of self-worth, one that is not connected to anyone other than you.

Adopting negative beliefs about yourself is not something for which you are to blame. It is a byproduct of the experiences to which you have been exposed and the strategies that you developed to survive to this day. You cannot be blamed if you have never had the chance to learn how to handle emotional health properly in order to thrive in your life. But, it *is* a new day, and you can now unlearn those bad habits and develop new, healthy strategies to thrive even during difficult times. This book will help you to realize those strategies and employ them in your life so that you will no longer be your own worst enemy. No matter where you are at right now, these strategies will help you to realize the reason behind your negative thinking and adopt new strategic mechanisms that will build your self-esteem, enhance the confidence you have in yourself, and achieve a state of inner peace you never thought possible.

You've taken the first step. You're seeking help. Take a moment to congratulate yourself. You've done a good thing, and you are worth this effort-- never doubt that. And now, it's time to take the next steps. Your new, healthier, happier life is waiting for you, and you deserve it. There's no greater reason than that to get started today.

Chapter One:
Why Self-Esteem and Confidence are Crucial

There's Self-Esteem, Then There's Confidence

You might be thinking that self-esteem and self-confidence are the same thing--and many people do use those terms interchangeably--but there is a very important difference between the two. Self-esteem refers to how you value yourself. This is often based on social norms, and you frequently measure yourself in comparison to other people. You might, for example, think, "I'm as intelligent and attractive as the next guy. Sure, I'm not a supermodel, but I'm not chopped liver either." Or, you might think, "I wish I was as witty as she is. I just can't think of things to say as fast as most people can." Both of these statements reflect a valuation of yourself in comparison to other people.

If you have high self-esteem, you are comfortable in your own skin. You're happy with who you are, regardless of how you might measure up to the next person. You can recognize and appreciate the gifts that other people might have, but--and this is important--you also recognize your own gifts, and you know that the gifts of other people do not detract from those of your own. You understand that you don't have to have the same gifts that everyone else has.

If you have low self-esteem, on the other hand, you will find yourself constantly not measuring up, and this can lead to depression as well as a sense of hopelessness. It can cause you to not even try because you think you will never succeed. You will also likely be submissive to other people's wishes because you don't believe you are capable of leading the way, even if we're talking about your own life. Additionally, you'll often find yourself feeling guilty as if you have done something wrong when, in fact, you've done nothing to be guilty about. You might think you have to prove you're as good as someone else, and for that reason, you likely will set an unrealistically high standard for perfection. That sets you up for failure, which reinforces the low opinion you already have of yourself. It's a vicious cycle. But, you might be thinking that you *do* have confidence in your ability to get things done. Ah, but confidence is a horse of a different color.

Self-confidence is how we view our ability to

do something, like overcome an obstacle or improve a skill. It's really about how you perceive your ability to get the job done. While it is true that completing tasks successfully can increase your self-confidence, and that can, in turn, increase your self-esteem, it is also possible that you can have high self-confidence and low self-esteem. You can believe that you can get the job done and simultaneously think you're not a good person.

On the other hand, you can have high self-esteem and low self-confidence. You can value yourself as a person but question your ability to do the job. This might be exemplified by people you know with high self-esteem who are extremely competent at a particular task (or even many tasks), but who are constantly questioning their work. They double and triple check themselves with every job they do. It's not that they think they're not intelligent enough to do the job, but they question their ability to get it done correctly. They constantly fear they will make a mistake. This is low self-confidence in action.

On the other end of the spectrum, people with high self-confidence can easily cross the line into arrogance. We tend to admire confident people, but what makes them confident is that they don't feel the need to advertise their skills. They know they have done the job well or that they have a particular talent, and they don't have to show off those skills in order to prove themselves. When people feel the need to flaunt their abilities, this is referred to as arrogance. In reality, it's another type of confidence, a false bravado that people project in order to cover what is likely their low self-esteem. These are the people who are loud, opinionated, and often abrasive in the presentation of their views. If someone feels the need to pander for adoration or is constantly looking to demonstrate they are the most knowledgeable or most capable individual, it likely indicates they secretly have a low opinion of themselves and are seeking external approval to prop up their self-image.

At this point, you might also be wondering about humility. Isn't being humble a good thing? Humility is defined as having a modest view of one's own importance. But, this doesn't mean exactly what it sounds like. It is not, in fact, encouraging low self-esteem. Rather, there is a difference between how you value yourself as a person and how you view your contributions in life. For example, you can know you are a good person and that you contributed in a meaningful way to the successful completion of a project, but at the same time, you can know that it was a team effort that got the job done. You can also understand that the completion of the project is more important than any one person's contribution alone.

To sum it up, self-esteem is the value you place on yourself, self-confidence is the view you have of your own ability to get something done, and humility is knowing that, while you know you are valuable and capable, there are more important things than your own accomplishments. Arrogance is when you feel the need to flaunt your abilities or accomplishments, and it often masks low self-esteem. But how do these things form? When do we develop our image of ourselves and our belief, or lack thereof, in our own abilities?

The Impact of Social Media on Self-Esteem and Confidence

Social media is ubiquitous in modern life. We check our Facebook page, Instagram, or Twitter feed first thing in the morning and numerous times throughout the day. We obsess over statuses and likes, and of course, those adorable little cat memes. But, it is important to be careful with social media because it can negatively affect the way you view your own life. In fact, one survey found that 60 percent of people who interacted on social media reported that it negatively affected their self-esteem, and 50 percent reported it had negatively affected their relationships (Silva 2017).

One of the problems with social media is that people tend to share only their highlights, and this creates an image of constant happiness that might not reflect reality. It creates an unrealistic appearance with which you might be comparing yourself. It appears all your 'friends' are always enjoying life and experiencing success, and you feel like you're not measuring up. But that's not reality. What you're not seeing is the behind the scenes struggles that they also go through as they face numerous challenges. They post that they got a new job, and you think, "Wow! How easy that was for them and now they're off on a new, exciting adventure." What they didn't post, however, were the numerous applications and perhaps some failed job interviews that came before they *finally* got the new job. You don't see the self-doubt they experienced about whether they would actually be able to find a new job. Also, it might not just be your friends' profiles that depress you. You might become depressed by your own profile if you realize that what you're posting is an illusion. You might think you're not living up to your own best self.

Does this mean you have to stop using social media? Maybe! You should take whatever means are necessary to prioritize building up your self-esteem and confidence. Maybe it doesn't mean you have to stop using social media, but consider taking a break from it while you focus on yourself if you feel it is holding you back. Whatever you decide to do, you need to realize that what you see on social media is the best face put forward by your many friends. It's like pictures in a photo album; you don't see the sad moments or the depressing and difficult times. You see the happy times, the successes, and the smiles. But, it's just a moment in someone's life, and it's usually just the best moments that they take a picture of, and then post on social media. That doesn't mean they don't have bad moments too--they're just not posting those in the same way you are likely not posting your own fears, anxieties, and difficulties in life. And, as with your 'physical' friends, you should seek out positive virtual friends and get rid of any virtual friends who try to tear you down. Virtual bullying can be even more damaging than what happens on the school playground since you can at least escape the playground. So, be careful about who you "friend"--make sure they're someone who will appreciate you! Remember, all the rules of building your self-esteem and self-confidence apply to the virtual realm as well as the physical.

How Insecurity, Self-Doubt and Fear Develop and Affect Your Life

Insecurity is defined as lacking confidence in oneself. It is something that people with a normal healthy level of self-confidence and healthy self-esteem can experience at some point in their life. We have all likely felt insecure at one point or another, but individuals with a healthy outlook on life usually resolve those feelings relatively quickly. The problem is that when it is not resolved within a relatively short period of time, it can do lasting damage. In fact, insecurity is linked to a number of mental health disorders, such as narcissism, anxiety, and addictive personalities (Blog 2019). So, what causes it?

Insecurity can result from a traumatic event, such as a divorce, a bankruptcy, or some other kind of loss. Also, an unpredictable environment or an upset in your daily routine can cause feelings of insecurity. If you're an individual with a healthy self-esteem and a normally healthy level of self-confidence, you likely will overcome the temporary feeling of insecurity brought about by a one-time event. However, if you are beset by numerous recurrences of unpredictable events and losses, it can damage your self-esteem and significantly lower your self-confidence. This can lead to feeling like you have a lack of direction in your life, and/or like you are invisible or being overlooked by the important people in your life. And, that can lead to depression, anxiety, and a whole host of other problems. You can begin to doubt everything you thought you knew to be true about yourself.

Another common source of insecurity is the events we experience in childhood. For example, if your parents pushed you to excel as a means of living vicariously through your success and without regard for your own desires, this can set you up to experience insecurity later in life. It often surfaces in adulthood. Additionally, a child's attachment bond--that is, their first love relationship which is normally formed with a primary caregiver--plays a very large role in the formation of insecurity (Babcock 2000). If your primary caregiver was not responsive to your needs or was abusive in response to your needs, you might have formed an insecure attachment. That can affect your ability to form lasting emotional connections, and of course, insecurity and anxiety will be a regular part of your life as a result. It makes sense--you learned early that life is unpredictable and you can't trust that your needs will be met, and that is because your primary caregiver did not respond to your needs adequately. Thus, you learned to fear life, and that can dramatically affect how you respond to life.

Aside from the direct interactions a primary caregiver might have with a child, there are also indirect influences. For example, if a child consistently hears their parents expressing negative feelings about themselves, that can also damage a child's self-esteem. If your mother was always saying, "I look terrible in this dress. I'm so fat," that can affect your own body image in a negative way. In fact, eating disorders are a common manifestation of insecurity. On the other hand, studies have found that even praise, when directed at the child personally versus the effort the child made, can also damage a child's self-esteem later in life (ScienceDaily, 2019). If, for example, you praise your child's abilities in soccer by saying, "You're so amazing," then later if the child doesn't do well, now he or she will think, "I'm not amazing now." Experts say in order to avoid this, you should praise the child's effort instead, something like, "You really worked hard on that." That way the child won't attach any feeling of self-worth to the activity. If they fail, it's not because they're not amazing, it's maybe just because they didn't work as hard at it as they should have.

Now that we've identified some of the sources of insecurity, let's examine how it can affect your life. There are numerous effects of persistent insecurity. It can affect your ability to form and maintain relationships because you will have difficulty sharing your emotions; you will be afraid your partner will not respond to your emotional needs in a loving way. It can also keep you from getting ahead in your work because your insecurity will prevent you from asking for more money, a promotion, or a particular job. And, it can lead to violent behavior. Research has shown that domestic abusers are likely to have experienced an insecure attachment in childhood (Babcock et al. 2000). And, the worst part is the turmoil that happens on the inside--the fear, the feeling of isolation, depression, anxiety, and a feeling of hopelessness--will constantly chip away at your self-esteem and confidence. It's no wonder that insecurity is at the root of addictive behaviors and mental disorders such as borderline and paranoid personalities, and schizophrenia (Blog 2019).

If you feel any or all of this, don't think you're alone. Some studies have shown that of the possible 80,000 thoughts we humans might have in one day, as much as 80 percent of those are negative. And, as much as 90 percent of those are repetitive thoughts (Millett, 2019). That means we are repetitively thinking mostly negative thoughts, and many of those are about ourselves. This is why it is so important to learn how to recognize your thoughts and how to change the negative into positive.

Part of the process is learning how to restore self-esteem and confidence. It is critical to learn to love and accept ourselves. To do that, we first have to understand the reasons behind our negative thoughts, and then we have to work at turning those negative thoughts into positive ones actively. That starts with recognizing the difference between the value we have of ourselves and our view of our ability to handle the ups and downs that life will bring. If we're able to restore our self-esteem and self-confidence successfully, we can achieve a happier, healthier, more balanced life.

What It Looks Like to Restore Self-Esteem and Confidence

Now that we have a definition for self-esteem and self-confidence, we can begin to look at ways to restore the value we place on our self and the confidence we have in our abilities. There are a number of steps you can take to start this process right away. Here are five steps you can begin today:

1. *Positive affirmations*

One step you can take is to improve your self-talk. In the chapters that follow, we'll look specifically at how to develop powerful, positive affirmations, but suffice it to say that thinking positively improves your mood, improves your self-confidence, and positive affirmations improve your self-esteem. We tend to believe the things that we say about ourselves repetitively, and so, if we make those things positive, we will eventually believe them. So, how do you accomplish this? Well, first of all, you can start small. Think about a recent success, be it in your professional or personal life, or think about something nice you did for someone--maybe you complimented them on how hard they've been working. Perhaps you told them it's paying off. Think about how complementing them makes you feel and why. Is it because you made them feel good? Well, that's a recent success. That's something to like about yourself, so say it out loud. Think about other things you like about yourself, and say those out loud. It often helps to say it in the form of a question too. For example, "Why am I so good at organizing my day?" or "Why are my legs so strong?" It turns out our brains are hard-wired to seek answers to questions without analyzing whether or not the question is even valid (Cascio et al. 2015), and so, when you ask why you're so good at something, your brain will look for those positive, affirming answers!

2. *Surround yourself with positive people*

We often surround ourselves with critics, or perhaps it's that we're so accustomed to having someone criticize us that we don't even realize the damage it is doing to our self-esteem. Maybe we think they're keeping us humble, but as we've seen, humility is not defined as low self-esteem, and our friends should be propping us up, not tearing us down. It's not that you want a bunch of sycophants to follow you around telling you that everything you do is perfect, but you do want people around you who recognize and appreciate your abilities. Those kinds of people will remind you of your value and help you through difficult times without blaming or demeaning you. They will be able to offer constructive suggestions in a loving way. They are the kind of people you want to seek out, and you should avoid those that would tear you down--you don't deserve that.

3. *Face your fears*

This is where you have to be honest with yourself about why you think you can't do something. Sit down and write out the reasons why you think you can't, and then, make another list of the reasons why you think you can. Be careful not to short change yourself because of low self-esteem. Be realistic about the can-dos and the can't-dos--it might even help to ask a good friend to brainstorm with you on this part, so you don't paint yourself in an unrealistic light. If you're realistic about it, chances are you'll have more reasons on the can-do list than you do on the can't-do list. And, when you see them written out like that, it makes it easier also to see ways to overcome those can't-do reasons. As you move forward with succeeding in doing things that scare you, you'll feel exponentially more confident in yourself.

One thing you'll want to do here to help ensure your success is to start with smaller goals and build up to the bigger ones. For example, make a list of five smaller goals that will get you closer to achieving a larger goal. If your goal is to run 10 miles each day, you might start by taking a five or ten-minute walk for one week and then increasing the time spent walking in the second week, and the third week, and so on. In no time, you'll be running those 10 miles daily. But, be sure to note the successes along the way, like running your first mile and then hitting the five-mile mark. Celebrate yourself for getting that far! The takeaway is that you should take it one step at a time and one day at a time--don't try to do too much at once, or you'll set yourself up for failure. And, don't let the perfect be the enemy of the good. Recognize that you may stumble along the way, but just trying to do tasks that you didn't think you could do in the first place is a great first step. When you have done a good job and achieved a goal, recognize that achievement, even if you think it's not perfect. Let the perfectionism go and appreciate the good.

4. *Visualize yourself as amazing!*

The American author Napoleon Hill said, "What the mind can conceive and believe, it can achieve." If you see yourself as a person you are proud of, and as someone who is able to overcome difficulties and achieve success in life, you will be that person. You might start by listing your strengths and weaknesses. If you're suffering from low self-esteem, it might be difficult to come up with your strengths at first, but think about even seemingly small, good things that you do. For example, maybe you love animals, and you take good care of your own pets, or perhaps you donate to charities that take care of strays or wild animals. That's a great thing! Or, maybe it's even more simple--maybe you greet the people in your neighborhood in a pleasant way when you see them. That's a strength, and surely, your neighbors would agree.

Even if you feel you have a lot of weaknesses, when you see the strengths you also have written down beside them, you understand that you have good qualities too. And, you can build on that. You can then set goals for improving some of the weaknesses you listed. For example, maybe you consider it a weakness that you procrastinate on projects to the point that it creates a lot of stress for you as you rush to get it done. So, you can set a goal to improve that by outlining a timeline for your current or next project, one that gives you plenty of time to complete it without creating anxiety. This will also allow you to check off those intermediate deadlines for different phases of the project, and checking those off will make you feel good. You can also create a journal to document the steps you take toward achieving your goals, and you can share your thoughts about the challenges you have overcome and those that are still yet to be overcome. As you go along, you will see that you are beginning to realize the amazing you!

5. *Take care of yourself*

This means taking care of yourself, both physically and mentally. Exercise at least a little bit each day. It will make you feel physically stronger, and that will help you feel mentally stronger too. Also, take care of yourself by setting boundaries. You need to learn how to say no when you are already too busy to take on another task, and you also have to be prepared to ask for what you need in order to take proper care of yourself. This could be something as simple as, "I need 30 minutes a day to myself, so I can exercise." Think carefully about what you need to feel physically and mentally fit, and then make the decision to prioritize getting those things. You are worth it!

As you begin to take these steps, you will start to see an improvement in both your self-confidence and your self-esteem. You will understand that you do, in fact, have many good qualities, and you are capable of achieving your goals. As your self-confidence increases, so will your self-esteem. You're on your way to becoming that amazing, capable person you visualized.

Chapter Summary

In this chapter, we have examined the difference between self-confidence and self-esteem. Self-confidence refers to your belief in your own ability to accomplish something, whereas self-esteem refers to how you value yourself as a human being. We discussed how it is that you can have confidence in your ability to do something, but still have low self-esteem. You can know, for example, that you are going to be able to fix that car, but still think you don't deserve to have a nice car, that you aren't worthy of it. Likewise, we examined how it is that a person can have high self-esteem and still lack confidence. You can believe in yourself, in your essential goodness, but still, lack confidence in your ability to complete a task or overcome an obstacle. You can know, for example, that you are a good, thoughtful boss, but still doubt your ability to successfully complete the task you must do in order to get a promotion.

We also examined the causes of insecurity that can lead to low self-esteem and impaired confidence. We discussed how repetitive traumatic events or losses could lead you to question your own abilities and worth, and we examined how childhood experiences can produce low self-esteem and low self-confidence. By examining the causes of our insecurities, we can understand that we are not to blame for developing the strategies we did in order to survive, but we also know that those strategies may no longer be serving us in a positive way. So, now we have the opportunity to develop new strategies that will boost and support our self-esteem and our confidence in our abilities. We discussed five specific steps you can take right now to begin this process. These included the use of positive affirmations, surrounding yourself with positive people, visualizing yourself as the person you want to be, facing your fears, and taking care of yourself. We also described the benefits of taking these steps.

In the next chapter, we are going to look more in-depth into the importance of positive and powerful affirmations. We'll look at the science behind how and why they work, and what the benefits are. We'll also look at a few examples of positive affirmations and answer some of the common questions. So, without further ado, let's look at how you can change your self-talk for the better.

Chapter Two:
The Importance of Positive and Powerful Affirmations

What are positive affirmations and do they work?

You might be thinking that positive affirmations are just wishing that you were better than you are, but that is not the case--they work! And, there's scientific evidence that they work. Before we look at that, let's define what we mean by positive affirmations. These are repetitive, positive statements or phrases that you can use to challenge any negative thoughts that show up or to simply encourage and uplift you throughout your day. To be effective, they have to follow a particular formula. You want to speak in the language of your brain. Your brain only speaks in the present tense. Therefore affirmations should only be in the present tense--e.g., "I will," or "I am." Next, they should only include positive words. There should be no can't(s) or don't(s) or other negative words or phrases. Finally, positive affirmations should be spoken as statements of truth--not I might or I could, but rather I am, or I will, or I can.

So, how does this affect your brain? Well, your brain is like a super-computer. It is processing so much information each second, and therefore, it has to take everything you say literally. *You* can communicate in the future or past tense, but your *brain* can't (Strecher 2015). Everything that is happening in the brain is happening right now, and so, it only understands the present tense. From a survival perspective, it makes sense. The brain has to be ready to respond on a moment's notice. When you think something, your brain prepares for the action that should result from that thought. It has to do a lot to get you prepared. For example, if it hears that you're frightened, it will key up certain physical responses that prepare you to either run away or fight. It doesn't know that the fear you might be expressing is a hypothetical fear of a future event. For example, "I'm afraid I won't get that job." The brain just hears "afraid" and responds accordingly. It's also true if you think something positive about a future event. If you think, for example, "I'm going to have such a good time on my vacation," the brain will hear good and cue up the proper response for something good, but it will be in the present moment. It won't wait until you're on your vacation. That's why affirmations need to be in the present tense and be addressing the present moment.

You also need to be sure to tell your brain what you want it to do and not what you don't want it to do. For example, if you think to yourself, "Don't be afraid, it's just a movie," your brain responds first to the straightforward concept of afraid. *You* know you said, *"Don't* be afraid," but your brain has to go through multiple steps to process the "don't be" part of that phrase (Strecher 2015). The problem is that even after your brain has gone through the multiple steps to interpret the "don't be" part of that thought, you haven't given it anything else to do other than to stimulate a fear response. You haven't thought, for example, "Be calm," and so, your brain can only interpret one action. You are basically telling your brain to be afraid, and you're likely doing it more than once. If, on the other hand, you were to say to yourself, "I am calm," your brain would process a completely different response, one that would result in a soothing physical state.

The literal nature of your brain is something that actually helps you. For example, if you are hungry, you don't have to then think separately about every sound, smell, and sight in your immediate environment to determine if it is food or not; your brain does that for you and focuses on food items. What that means is that your brain is constantly on alert. It is always looking for clues with regard to what it should filter in accordance with your needs. This is where you can actually take control of the process. Up until now, you might have been unconsciously directing your brain toward negative responses because of unresolved fears and doubts that you have yet to deal with. But, if you change that, and instead, feed your brain positive affirmations, it will activate the responses you need to be wildly successful. In fact, there are numerous benefits to using these affirmations. Here are just a few of the ways that positive affirmations can help you:

• They can raise your self-esteem and confidence.

• They can help you reduce (or stop) your negative self-talk and replace that with positive messages.

• They can boost your problem-solving abilities.

• They can increase your creativity and insight.

• They can improve your performance and productivity.

• They can help you overcome bad habits.

• They can help you finish projects.

• They can help you become more physically active.

• They can help you improve your mental and physical health.

• They can help you improve your interpersonal relationships.

That's a long list, and the great thing about it is that affirmations really can help you in all of these areas. But, you have to craft them carefully and use them often. Repetition is important. Before we discuss how to use affirmations, however, let's look at some examples of powerful, positive affirmations.

Benefits of Daily Affirmations

As we have discussed, positive, present-tense statements addressing the present moment are how you should phrase your affirmations (and we'll look at this more in the subsequent chapters), but repetition is the key to success. This is because repeating thoughts, or even activities, strengthen the connections in the brain for those positive responses. That means by consistently repeating positive affirmations, you'll need less energy, be calmer, and you'll have more focus on the task you're performing because your brain has strong connections in place to rapidly stimulate the appropriate physical response. Think about the adage, "It's like riding a bicycle." That saying means that something you know how to do will come back to you when you go to it anew, even if it has been a long time. Why is that true? Why can you go years without riding a bicycle, but the moment you get back on that bike, you can ride like you've been doing it every day since you first learned? Well, the reason is that the repetition of the activity over the years in your youth strengthened those connections in the brain. The same is true for positive affirmations. When you repeat them daily, and in fact, several times each day, those connections in the brain are strengthening. The brain is learning to respond more quickly to what will eventually become routine, common, and positive responses. Once those strengthened, positive pathways are in place, like the bicycle, you never forget. Let's look at a few examples.

Examples of Positive Affirmations

We've discussed some of the elements of positive affirmations. They need to be framed in the present tense and using positive rather than negative words. But, if you feel like the affirmation is a lie, then that will create tension, which may also be helpful. An example might be someone who wants to lose weight. One affirmation could be, "I love my body," but if the person doesn't (and of course, they know if they don't), then it feels like a falsehood. But, there is something to be said for repeating this falsehood. It can create motivation to change what you don't like so that the affirmation becomes true. It can motivate you to do something about it. In fact, if the affirmation makes you squirm a little, that discomfort might signal it is exactly the affirmation you need. The bottom line is that you will either change the affirmation to make it more comfortable or change that area of your life to make the affirmation true. If you do the latter, you can dramatically improve your life. With that in mind, let's take a look at some great examples of well-phrased positive affirmations (Mindvalley Blog, 2019):

- **I accept myself** - this is a great one for anyone, whether they are unhappy with their weight or other aspects of their body or not - it is simply self-acceptance.

- **I know myself, and I am true to myself** - this is a good one for everyone as well, even if they feel they have certain weaknesses, this can hold true and be an impetus for improvement;

- **I eat well and take care of myself** - this is something that can also hold true no matter your weight or current state of health, and it is good motivation.

- **I exercise and get plenty of rest** - again, if this is not as true as you would like, it can provide you with motivation.

- **I commit to learning new things** - this is a good one for keeping our mind active as well as our body.

- **I never give up** - this is a great one for helping to overcome setbacks.

- **My happy thoughts help me create a healthy body** - this helps you keep a positive attitude and use that to create a healthy body.

- **I am in perfect health** - this can help you as you overcome physical injuries;

- **Wellness is my body's natural state** - this reaffirms the natural physical state of your body, and can help you to regain your health.

There are also positive affirmations designed for specific situations, such as work or love life affirmations. A few work-related affirmations are as follows (Mindvalley Blog, 2019):

- I love the work I do every day.

- I have my dream job.

- I am a valued employee.

- I attract new clients.

- I efficiently get my work done.

- My job brings me financial abundance.

- I am excited about my work.

- My boss and my clients value the work I do.

- I make good decisions easily.

- I radiate success.

And, here are a few directed at your love life:

- I am attractive.

- I am a kind, compassionate partner.

- I forgive my partner and myself easily.

- My life is filled with love.

- I am sexy.

- I base my relationships on love and mutual respect.

- My words are kind and loving.

- My romantic relationship is healthy and long-lasting.

- I attract kind, loving, and respectful partners.

- I am attracted to kind, loving, and respectful partners.

- I radiate love, and that love is reflected back at me.

Notice how all of these examples are in the present tense, and they all involve positive statements that reaffirm your self-worth, your self-confidence, and they "talk" to your brain in a way so that your brain can respond with positive physical and mental preparations in the present moment. They give your brain something to do, and they are uplifting as well. You can also transform these affirmations into a question. This was mentioned in Chapter 1. It helps because it stimulates your brain to look for those uplifting answers. This would look something like the following:

1. Why do I accept myself so completely?

2. Why do I attract kind, loving, and respectful partners?

3. Why am I so amazing at my job?

4. Why am I so sexy?

This stimulates your brain to find answers, and the answers to these kinds of questions are going to be good. You accept yourself so completely because you know yourself to be good and true to your values. You attract kind, loving, and respectful partners because you are a kind, loving, and respectful partner. You are amazing at your job because you are efficient, intelligent, and a great problem-solver. You are sexy because you appreciate your body, you stay healthy, you eat right, and you exercise. Your brain will find these answers for you, and they will improve your self-esteem and your self-confidence. One caveat with regard to interrogative affirmations--notice that you aren't asking, "Am I sexy?" You are asking, "*Why am I* so sexy?" You're not asking, "Do I accept myself," you're asking, "Why do I accept myself so completely?" You're affirming the good as part of the question, and asking your brain to give you all the wonderful reasons why you are so good.

So, we've defined positive affirmations, we've discussed a little bit about how they interact with your brain, and we've examined a few examples of powerful affirmations. Now, let's look at the science behind them.

The Science Behind Positive Affirmations

Researchers (Kan et al. 2015) have conducted experiments on the effects of positive affirmations on work performance. They found that if you spend just a few minutes thinking about your best qualities--for example, "I am intelligent, I am persuasive, I am calm, I am a good worker"--these affirmations can significantly improve your chances of success with a task (such as meeting), they can calm your nerves, and they can boost your confidence. In fact, the study showed that underperformance *disappears* when the individual has had an opportunity to self-affirm, and these experiments were conducted on individuals in high-pressure settings. Furthermore, in one study conducted to assess how self-affirmation affects those chronically stressed, underperforming individuals, **the results showed that one brief self-affirmation exercise not only improved the problem-solving abilities of these individuals but also increased their creativity and insight** (Cresswell et al. 2013). And, that's only one, brief exercise! Imagine what daily repetition can do for you.

Positive affirmations have also been used to treat individuals with mental health conditions that include low self-esteem and depression (Moore 2019). Not only do the studies confirm the physical changes in the brain that positively affect self-evaluation, but they also show that with increased self-worth, individuals are more likely to do what is necessary to improve their own well-being. This can include exercising or eating more healthy foods. When you think you're worth it--and you are--you take better care of yourself. A study by two researchers at the University of California, Berkeley, and Cornell

University found that positive affirmations give us a broader perspective on self-threats (Critcher and Dunning 2015). This explains many of the benefits derived from affirmations. What they found is that when we engage in positive affirmations, we get a broader perspective on the self and the role any threat plays. The affirmations effectively make the threat seem more narrow in relation to the entire concept of the self. The result of that is that the threat is less all-defining of the self. In other words, we can more easily see and understand that even if we did make some kind of mistake, that is not the whole of who we are; it is merely one small part, and that one small part does not negate our essential goodness. Understanding this means that we will respond in a less defensive manner to these types of threats, and this reduces our stress and helps us integrate the information obtained from the self-threat to improve ourselves as well as maintain healthy self-esteem and confidence.

For those science nerds out there (myself among them), there are specific changes in the brain that positive affirmations create. Researchers specifically found an increase in activity in the medial prefrontal cortex and the posterior cingulate cortex where the brain's self-processing takes place. The ventral medial prefrontal cortex and the vertical striatum where self-evaluation takes place also showed an increase in activity, and the increased activity in all of these areas was demonstrated to be in relation to future-oriented core values rather than past ones (Cascio et al, 2016). This means that positive affirmations help us to make ourselves into the people we truly know ourselves to be; these systems help us to look forward instead of constantly looking backward and beating ourselves up over our past mistakes. And, the research also found that the neural changes in these areas stimulated a change in sedentary behavior whereby individuals became more physically active in association with an improved concept of self-worth (Falk et al. 2015).

In sum, scientific research consists of numerous studies that confirm the mental and physical benefits of self-affirmations. They show that among the benefits are reduced stress (which has numerous health benefits), a broader perspective on the self, which helps us to understand our complexity and to not focus on our past mistakes, increased self-esteem and confidence, improved problem-solving abilities as well as creativity and insight, and an increase in physical activity (which also has numerous health benefits). That's an extensive list of benefits to positive, powerful affirmations. Still, you may have a lot of questions about positive affirmations, and you wouldn't be the first, so let's look at the answers to some of the common questions.

Answers to Common Questions on Affirmations

Several common questions asked about affirmations have already been answered in this chapter.

- Yes, there is actual science behind the use of positive affirmations, and numerous studies clearly demonstrate the physical and mental benefits (Cascio et al. 2015; Cohen and Sherman 2014; Cresswell et al. 2013; Critcher and Dunning 2015; Falk et al. 2015; Kan et al. 2015).

- Yes, positive affirmations can help boost your self-esteem, self-confidence, and they can help you to fight depression as well as other mental disorders.

- They do work best if you say them every day, and in fact, you should practice affirmations at least 3 - 5 times each day. And, as we'll see in the chapters that follow, you should repeat each affirmation three times before moving on to the next one. It's also helpful if you write them down in a journal and practice saying them to yourself in a mirror.

A few common questions that have not been addressed yet include the following:

1. Can I use affirmations to improve my sleep?

> Many people who suffer from insomnia also suffer from anxiety. So, if you use positive affirmations to reduce anxiety, that can also help with anxiety-induced insomnia. Additionally, you can incorporate your positive affirmations into your meditation practice. Meditation is commonly used to help improve sleep, and by incorporating positive affirmations, you can further alleviate anxiety and improve the relaxation component of meditation. That translates into a better, deeper, more relaxed sleep.

2. Are positive affirmations the same as positive mantras?

> There is a difference between mantras and affirmations, though you often see the two terms used interchangeably. Mantras, however, typically refer to sacred words, sounds, or verses that carry more of a spiritual meaning than affirmations. They tend to have spiritual significance to the speaker and can be thought of essentially as distillations of spiritual wisdom.

Positive affirmations, on the other hand, are designed to encourage positive, happy thoughts for the speaker. They do not have a particular spiritual meaning in the traditional sense.

3. How do I create positive, powerful affirmations?

Well, I'm glad you asked that question, and that will be the subject of subsequent chapters. But, as we have noted, a few characteristics of powerful affirmations include the fact that they are in the present tense, they don't include negative words, they should address the present moment, and they should give your brain something positive to do, like look for all the reasons you're so great. We'll take those specific characteristics in the following chapters and help you to understand exactly how to create your own powerful affirmations that will restore your sense of inner peace and self-acceptance, boost your self-esteem and confidence, and give you the positive outlook you need as you confront the challenges of life.

Chapter Summary

In this chapter, we have defined affirmations and discussed some of the basic components of power, positive affirmations. We have also discussed how your brain processes information, and the importance of structuring affirmations using positive words, the present tense, and language that relates to the present moment. In response to such affirmations, the brain is able to initiate physical reactions that correspond to the nature of the affirmation. For example, "I am calm," tells the brain to initiate a cascade of physical responses related to being calm. Therefore, you will be calm.

We also examined some of the benefits of positive affirmations, specifically how they can help you be more successful in your career or job, how they can help with your interpersonal relationships, and how they can help you with the relationship you have with yourself. That is, they can help you to boost your self-esteem and self-confidence. Additionally, we examined a few examples of powerful, positive affirmations. We looked at some general examples of affirmations as well as some that are specific to your work life and your love life. We then discussed how these affirmations could be restated as a question that both affirms the positive nature of the affirmation and compels the brain to look for all of the positive reasons why the affirmation is true.

Lastly, we discussed the scientific studies that have demonstrated the power of positive affirmations. We discussed how daily repetition of affirmations can create new neural pathways in the brain that reinforce the good feelings generated by those positive messages, and we discussed the studies that show even one exercise using positive affirmations can reduce stress and increase your chances of success. These studies clearly demonstrate how and why affirmations work.

In the next chapter, we'll look at numerous examples of affirmations for self-worth, self-esteem, and self-confidence.

Chapter Three: Powerful Affirmations

The following powerful affirmations should be repeated three times before moving on to the next one. Remember that you are creating stronger neural pathways for responding to these positive words (Raj, 2019; Aham-adi, 2018; Camp, 2016).

Let's begin with some general positive affirmations:

1. I am a powerful creator.

2. I create the life I want.

3. I am OK as I am.

4. I accept and love myself.

5. I am unique. I feel good about being alive and being me.

6. Life is fun and rewarding.

7. Amazing opportunities exist for me in every aspect of my life.

8. I am successful right now.

9. I am passionate.

10. I am outrageously enthusiastic and inspire others.

11. I am calm and peaceful.

12. I have unlimited power at my disposal.

13. I love challenges; they bring out the best in me.

14. I replace "I have to" with "I choose to."

15. I choose to be happy right now. I love my life.

16. I appreciate everything I have. I live in joy.

17. I am courageous. I am willing to act.

18. I am positive and optimistic.

19. I believe things always work out for the best.

20. It's easy to make friends. I attract positive and kind people into my life.

21. It's easy to meet people. I create positive and supportive relationships.

22. I am confident.

23. I trust myself.

24. I never give up.

25. I choose to be happy in every moment.

26. I am flexible and adapt to challenges and experiences.

27. I always expect the best and think positively.

28. I am strong. I live a powerful life.

29. My life is both beautiful and rewarding.

30. I have been blessed with health and happiness.

31. I appreciate the things I have. I rejoice in the love I receive.

32. I am successful. I live with joy and abundance.

33. I am in full control of my life, and I am at peace with myself.

34. My growth is a continuous process. I am not stuck.

35. I believe in my skills and abilities.

36. I have great ideas and always make meaningful contributions.

37. I receive all the useful information I need to succeed.

Let's look at some affirmations that speak directly to your self-esteem (Raj, 2019; Aham-adi, 2018; Camp, 2016):

1. I love who I am.

2. I am always growing and developing.

3. My opinions resonate with who I am.

4. I deserve to be happy and successful.

5. I have the power to change myself.

6. I easily forgive and understand others and their motives.

7. I make my own choices and decisions.

8. I choose to pursue my dreams and give priority to my desires.

9. I choose happiness no matter what my circumstances are.

10. I am flexible and open to change in every aspect of my life.

11. I act with confidence.

12. It is enough to have done my best.

13. I am enough.

14. I deserve to be loved.

15. I have high self-esteem.

16. I love and respect myself.

17. I am a great person.

18. My thoughts and opinions are valuable.

19. I am confident that I can achieve anything.

20. I have something special to offer the world.

21. Others like and respect me.

22. I am a wonderful human being.

23. I am worthy of having high self-esteem.

24. I believe in myself.

25. I deserve to feel good about myself.

26. I know I can achieve anything.

27. I respect myself deeply.

28. I am unique. No one else can offer what I can to this world.

29. I am solution-driven. Every challenge is a chance to grow.

30. Love supports me in expected and unexpected ways.

31. I live present in every moment. I enjoy life to the fullest.

32. I have the power to change myself.

33. Only I am responsible for making my choices and decisions.

34. I give priority to my desires.

35. I choose happiness.

36. I am flexible and open to new experiences.

Let's look at a few more affirmations related to self-worth (Raj, 2019; Aham-adi, 2018; Camp, 2016):

1. I am a unique and very special person.

2. I love myself more each day.

3. I approve of myself.

4. I care about myself

5. My work gives me pleasure.

6. I give praise freely.

7. I am respected by others.

8. I rejoice in my worth.

9. I attract praise.

10. I deserve good in my life.

11. I appreciate myself.

12. Each day I am becoming more self-confident.

13. I breathe in confidence.

14. I acknowledge my own self-worth.

15. I am worthy of all the good things that happen in my life.

16. I am confident with my life plan and the way things are going.

17. I deserve the love I am given.

18. I let go of the negative feelings about myself and accept all that is good.

19. I stand by my decisions. They are sound and reasoned.

Chapter Summary

In this chapter, we have seen several examples of powerful, positive affirmations you can use to boost your self-esteem, your self-confidence, and your sense of self-worth. These affirmations give you the power to thrive.

In the next chapter, we will discuss inner peace and self-acceptance. We will examine what it is that disturbs our sense of inner peace, and look at the practical actions we can take to restore and maintain a stable sense of inner peace. We will also discuss how to achieve unconditional self-acceptance. It starts with compassion for yourself and learning how to forgive yourself. The process involves setting clear intentions and understanding that we must able to "present our imperfect human selves to the world" while, at the same time, acknowledging our essential goodness. You might think you can't ever fully accept or forgive yourself, but the next chapter will present you with the tools that will allow you to do just that.

Chapter Four: Inner Peace and Self-Acceptance

What Disturbs Inner Peace?

Inner peace is a state of psychological or spiritual calm, even despite the presence of stress. It allows you to stay strong in the face of challenges, and if it is lost, you experience a near-constant state of anxiety. What can you do to get it back when it is lost? When we discuss how to re-establish inner peace and self-acceptance, it is helpful to examine what it is that actually disturbs us in the first place--that is, how we can lose it to begin with. We all have times when our inner tranquility is disturbed--perhaps we're working on a particularly frustrating problem, and we dwell on it too much, or perhaps we are feeling strong emotions, and that can cause us to become easily angered--but it is when we have trouble overcoming those short-term disturbances that it becomes a real problem. When negative emotional states, like jealousy, anger, sadness, or stress, become constant in our lives, then they can do real damage to our inner peace, our self-acceptance, our self-esteem, and our confidence. Maybe you think, "Well, I've just got a short fuse," or "I'm soul-sick," but these kinds of justifications for your negative emotions are self-destructive, and they indicate emotional dysfunction. On the other hand, if you keep your negative emotions inside, as many in our culture are taught to do (particularly men), that is inherently self-abusive. You are only damaging yourself with that kind of behavior, and the damage is real. It takes a toll on our health and our state of mind. As we have discussed in previous chapters, there is real science behind the benefits of positive self-affirmations, and likewise, there is real science behind the negative effects of emotional dysfunction. Chronic stress upsets the body's hormonal balance, negatively affects the immune system and depletes the brain of the chemicals required for *Are you overly anxious? Do you find yourself worrying all the time?* It's something we all learn to do. Our parents and our fear-based culture have taught us that we should worry. People often say to us, "Aren't you worried about that?" They reinforce not only our own anxiety but the fact that we should be anxious. It's interesting to note that not once has worrying solved a problem. It only results in causing more stress. If you've got a problem, and you can do something about it, then instead of worrying, do what you can to solve the problem. If you can't do anything about it, then worrying is not going to help. What are you worrying about? You are worrying about something that hasn't happened yet. "I'm worried I'll lose my job," or "I'm worried something bad will happen." But, these things haven't happened yet. Worrying is like paying interest on a loan you may never get. You haven't lost your job yet, you're just worried you will-- and that could cause you to do things that will make that fear come true! We convince ourselves that by worrying, we can somehow reduce the pain we will feel if the thing we're worried about would actually happen. But, by doing that, we're not reducing the pain; we're only prolonging it. A better strategy is to stay in the moment and experience the emotions that come as a result of what is actually happening. If you find yourself slipping into a state of anxiety, it can be helpful to think something like, "I am calm," or "I love a challenge."

Here some good questions to ask yourself:

1. *Do I negatively judge others and find it difficult to forgive them?*

This is another dysfunctional emotional pattern. You really are only hurting yourself when you judge harshly and withhold forgiveness. It's very easy to make snap judgments about other people, and it's even easier to judge ourselves. Most of the time, the behaviors that trigger our harshest judgments are based out of the fear that we are just like that. It's our shadow self--that side of our personality that contains the parts we don't want to admit we have--that we are truly judging; it's just the other person that is showing us what that behavior looks like. And, because we find it so difficult to forgive ourselves, we also withhold forgiveness for them. When we face those fears hidden among the shadows of our mind, we realize that, in the words of the 16th-century preacher John Bradford, "There, but for the grace of God go I." Usually, when you know the complete picture, you have a lot more compassion for people you would otherwise judge unfairly. Everyone has their own private challenges that aren't visible, and so the outside observer only sees the external wrong-doing. When we more fully understand the nature of those private challenges, we are able to have compassion for the person's behaviors. And, it's that compassion that can help us to forgive both ourselves and others.

2. *Do I hold on to guilt?*

When we feel guilty, it's a signal that we have done something that goes against our conscience. But, holding on to guilt does nothing to resolve the situation we feel guilty about, and it is a corrosive emotion to keep inside long-term, and it needs to be resolved quickly before it does lasting damage. We have a tendency to wallow in shame and regret, but we need to realize that everyone makes mistakes, and some mistakes have grave consequences. We have to face our mistakes, acknowledge at least to ourselves that we don't like what we did--while at the same time acknowledging that we are not our actions--and take whatever steps are possible to make amends. Once a mistake has been made, no amount of guilt, shame, or regret will take it back. So, what do you do? Well, the first thing you should do is to learn from your mistakes. For this, you have to reflect on what it is you did wrong and why you think it is wrong--why do you feel guilty? To show remorse, you want to take corrective actions, if those are possible. Perhaps, it's as simple as an apology, or you may have to pay for your mistake with money or maybe even something like time in prison. But, even the prisoner can learn from his or her mistakes and grow into a better person. You do this by resolving not to repeat the mistake you made, and take action to ensure you can keep that promise. That means building new strategies moving forward that will keep you from making the same mistake again. And, whatever you do, stop beating yourself up. Acknowledge your mistake, take corrective actions, and build new strategies, all the while keeping in mind your essential truth. You're a worthwhile person who made a mistake. Later in this chapter, we'll talk more about how to forgive yourself and move forward with your life.

3. *Am I sad and depressed more often than not?*

It's normal to feel blue occasionally, and certainly, the loss of a loved one can provoke an extended period of grief, but when sadness, depression, or grief become constants in our emotional state, that can indicate emotional dysfunction. Of course, depression can be indicated by a chemical imbalance in the brain, and there are drugs to treat it, but the drugs don't treat the low self-esteem and harsh self-judgment that accompany and deepen the depression. This is often representative of our inability to accept and embrace our past for what it is and how it has shaped our lives. We have to do that hard work as part of accepting ourselves and understanding our own inherent value as human beings. A good first step in that process is powerful, positive affirmations.

4. Do I often feel negative feelings like jealousy, frustration (especially with small things), and frequently feeling offended?

If any or all of these feelings are dominating your life, they can indicate emotional dysfunction that greatly disturbs your sense of inner peace. While all of these feelings can be normal on occasion, they become dysfunctional when they dominate your emotional state for extended periods of time. Jealousy represents a negative and often unrealistic judgment we have made of others, and we frequently make that kind of judgment because of our own insecurity. If we truly understand our own self-worth, we have no need to be jealous of other people. Frequent frustration, particularly with small things, often indicates a deeply held anger or sadness that you have yet to deal with. And, frequently feeling offended only results in putting yourself through suffering because of the negative behavior of others. They are the ones who did something to offend you, so why are you suffering for it? It might be because you're judging them, and as we have discussed, that is frequently reflective of your own harsh self-judgment.

All of these emotional states are normal every now and again, but it's when they become a constant part of our mental state that they become a problem. These emotional patterns are extremely disruptive to our sense of inner peace. They can also negatively affect our self-esteem and self-confidence. So, what can you do about them? Let's look at some practical actions you can take to produce and maintain inner peace. happiness (Taking Charge of Your Health & Wellbeing, 2019). So, how do you identify if you are emotionally dysfunctional?

Let's look at the emotional patterns that can easily disturb your inner peace:

Practical Actions to Produce and Keep Inner Peace

We have looked at some of the things that can disturb your inner peace, but now let's talk about specific, practical actions you can take to produce and maintain a sense of inner peace. Here are 20 practical actions you can take to help establish inner peace and maintain it:

Use positive, powerful affirmations on a daily

basis--and repeat each affirmation three times before moving on to the next one. We have discussed at length how these affirmations can help boost your self-esteem and self-confidence. Doing so helps you to establish and maintain that inner peace you seek.

1. *Leave nothing unresolved*--clear up the unresolved issues in your life. These unresolved issues can sap your energy and bring you down. You might not be able to resolve everything at once, but you can take the first step. That will make you feel better and get the ball rolling. You'll feel a great sense of relief just to get started.

2. *Surrender and accept what is*--this is, perhaps, the most difficult thing to do. The simple fact is that there are things beyond your control. It's hard to accept that, but when you arrive at the realization that you have done everything you can do, the next step is to surrender and accept what is. Take a deep breath and detach yourself from the situation. If there is a solution that you can put into effect, it will often appear when you step back and let go.

3. *Take responsibility for your reactions*-- you don't control how other people behave. You do, however, control your own actions and reactions. If you react in anger, take responsibility for that, and step away from the situation until you can re-establish a sense of calm. Remember the affirmation that begins with "I choose..." and choose to be calm and react in a constructive, positive way. To do this successfully, you have to decide who it is you want to be and resolve to maintain that integrity in all situations. Mentally prepare yourself to be calm, no matter what.

4. *Don't ignore your feelings--be aware of them and be sensitive to them--*your feelings matter, and you should not push them away. That only buries the problem, and they will bubble back up when you least want them to do so. Take time to understand what is provoking your feelings. Try this the next time you feel something uncomfortable--stop, turn around, and say, as if speaking to a child, "I see you there. Can you tell me why you're feeling sad or mad or frustrated?" Usually, you'll get an insight as to why, and when you do, accept that by saying, "I understand why you feel that way. That is a sad situation or a frustrating situation, and I don't blame you. You have every right to have those feelings. I'm here to help resolve these feelings, and we will be okay." This exercise acknowledges the feeling (I see you there), explores the reason (can you tell me why), and accepts that not only is that feeling valid, it is understandable given the circumstances. It also is you giving loving support to yourself.

5. *Tell the truth, the whole truth, and nothing but the truth*--resist lying, editing, or putting your own spin on something. Just be real. The Buddhists say that if you have something to say, consider first if it is true, then consider is it something that you need to say, and if it is, say it in a gentle, kind way.

6. *Know your higher self*--take the time to learn what you value, what your goals, your joys, and your passions truly are. These form the foundation of your integrity. You also need to be able to distinguish your higher self from your egoic mind, your needs, and your past. You are not your past. You experienced your past, but that is not who you are. You are a strong person who survived your past.

7. *Kick the adrenaline habit*--we have become a culture of adrenaline junkies. We seek out that rush that comes when we have a looming deadline, or some emergency arises. But, it is so important to slow down and find balance in your life in order to establish inner peace.

8. *Know what rattles you*--if you know what pushes your buttons, then you can really start to know yourself. Why do you react that way? Understanding that can help you heal those old wounds and finally be free of their insidious influence on the choices you make in your life.

Once you understand the roots of those feelings, you can deal with them in a healthy way.

9. *Do sweat the small stuff*--this doesn't mean worry about it, but rather pay attention to the imbalance that might show up in your life, the relationships that cause you frustration, and the unresolved problems. Shining a light on these areas of your life is the doorway to deep realizations and long-term healing.

10. *Prioritize* *peace over performance*--do you want to look back on your life only to find that you spent the majority of it running around completing long to-do lists or do you want to know that you genuinely lived in and appreciated your life, your friends, your family, and yourself? Take time to appreciate what you have, who you are, and who you love. When it comes time to look back on your life, you'll be happy you did, and the peace you create for yourself will spread to others making the world a better place.

11. *Find relaxation techniques and use them--*this is imperative for self-care. It doesn't matter what helps you relax--long walks, yoga, meditation, soaking in a tub. Whatever it is, do it and stick to it. You need this to create the inner peace you're seeking, and remember, you are worth it.

12. *Get rid of clutter*--the less clutter you see on the outside, the less clutter you will feel on the inside. Get rid of things that don't serve you anymore. By keeping your space tidy and free from clutter, you'll create a peaceful environment in which you can relax and foster an inner sense of peace.

13. *Disconnect and escape*--in our technology-laden world, it can be hard to disconnect, but it is important to take the time to do so in order to remember who you are without it. Our technology is useful, but it's also a distraction from living our lives. Instead of watching videos of people hiking in the mountains, go out and take a walk yourself. Look at the real-life that is around you, fill your senses with the smells and sounds of your environment, and take the time to live your life. This will help you to not only live your life but also to love your life.

14. *Get enough sleep*--this is another important self-care tip. When you're mind is groggy, it's easy to fall into negative thinking. And, nothing goes as smoothly when you're grumpy. Additionally, sleep deprivation leads to all sorts of negative health consequences, such as high blood pressure, impaired glucose control, and increased inflammation (Healthysleep.med.harvard.edu, 2019).

15. *Resist guilt*--as we noted, it is a negative emotion that does nothing to solve problems. Do what you can to take corrective steps, forgive yourself for anything you did wrong, and move on with your life.

16. *Be grateful for your life*--you might even create a gratitude journal. Each day, write down five things you're grateful for, and when you do, you'll begin to see all the good things in your life.

17. *Play*--remember when you couldn't wait for recess to go out and run around? Well, that's still a good strategy. Every day, take a little time to play like the child you once were. Engage in your favorite hobby, do an exercise that doesn't feel like exercising--like dancing--or even just play like a kid. Do the hula hoop, jump rope, or swing on a swing. Whatever it is, it should be something fun. It will bring joy back into your life!

18. *Connect with other people*--you might be an introvert, but it is still good to have some connections with other people. You'll live longer if you do (News, 2019), and it's always nice to have a few good friends in your corner. One caveat--be sure they are friends. These should be people who lift you up rather than tear you down.

19. *Don't compare yourself to other people*--remember that the qualities of other people, the talents they have, the material things they have, do not, in any way, detract from who you are or what your talents are or what you have. Celebrate your friends' successes, and you'll find there's nothing they have that is really important that you don't also have.

Now that we've identified some practical steps you can take to re-establish a sense of inner peace, let's turn to the topic of self-acceptance.

Self-Acceptance Begins with Intentionality

"Because true belonging only happens when we present our authentic, imperfect selves to the world, our sense of belonging can never be greater than our level of self-acceptance."—Brene Brown

This quote by Brene Brown defines the essence of self-acceptance. You're not perfect, and you're not going to be, but that doesn't mean you're not good, kind, loving, joyful, and many other good things. It is through accepting our authentic selves that we can feel as though we belong in the world. Self-acceptance, however, doesn't mean accepting who we want to be; it means accepting who we are, warts and all. It starts with intentionality. That means that you need to be very intentional with regard to how you think. And, you should be intentionally building yourself up. That doesn't mean you ignore your faults, but you accept that you have those faults while at the same time acknowledging they are not the whole of who you are. Then, you can be intentional with the steps you take to change them.

For example, maybe you feel like your propensity to be sarcastic is a fault. The first thing you do is accept that about yourself--" I am sarcastic." You might even praise yourself for having a quick wit. It might also help if you understand why you are sarcastic. This can mean being willing to be vulnerable with yourself. This allows you to see who you really are (rather than who you want to be) and gain insight into why you are that way. Maybe, for example, sarcasm was something you experienced in your own childhood, and you adopted it as your strategy too. But now that you understand that, you can take charge, and you can set the intention to use that quick wit differently. You might intentionally think, for example, "I have a quick wit. Sometimes I use that wit in a sarcastic way. It's good to be so witty, but now I am choosing to start using my wit in a healthier, kinder way." You see how you're accepting how you are, and you're also making a conscious choice about how you want to change something about yourself. The power is in your hands, and you're using it to create the life you want.

You should be equally intentional in the actions you take. Don't go places where you feel uncomfortable, don't do things you don't like to do, and don't bring things into your life that you don't want to be there. Sometimes you can't avoid doing something you don't necessarily want to do, but you can set the intention to do it well and quickly so that you can move on to something you enjoy. And, for those things under your control, you can make better choices for yourself. Part of doing this means you need to be mindful of how you're feeling. You need to be aware of those uncomfortable feelings when they come up, and you need to address them rather than shutting them down. That will allow you to understand the source of your discomfort. It generates compassion, and that is the way to heal those old wounds.

Compassion and Forgiveness for Yourself

Forgiving ourselves of what we perceive as shortcomings is a difficult thing to do. We often hold ourselves to an unrealistic standard. But, developing compassion for ourselves and learning to forgive ourselves is a powerful healing process. To start, we must develop compassion by recognizing that the human experience is one of learning and growing. As part of this process, we often fall short of our aspirations. Think about something you have done that you don't like, something for which you are judging yourself harshly. Now, think about what you would say if a good friend of yours came to you and told you they had done just what you did. You likely would be far more compassionate with them than you are with yourself. Now, try saying to yourself what you would say to your good friend. Give yourself the compassion you deserve.

Try this exercise--get to a place where you can sit quietly without any distractions, and think about something you did that you feel guilty about. Let yourself experience the feelings you have as you consider this thing you did, and remind yourself you are not your feelings; you are much more. In this way, you can separate yourself from the action you took and the results that ensued. Allow yourself to understand why you did what you did with compassion. If you acted out of fear, see the small child in you who was afraid and comfort him or her. And, give yourself the gift of forgiveness. Express your forgiveness out loud so that all of you can hear it. Now envision something you love dearly--for example, a pet, a child, or another person. Let that love rise up inside you and flood into your experience. Envision that love as a glowing source of white light in your heart and allow it to spread throughout the entirety of your body. Say again, out loud, that you forgive yourself for judging yourself as unworthy. Close this exercise by appreciating how strong you are to be willing to engage in what can be a very difficult activity and give yourself love. In this way, you can free yourself from the self-judgment that restricts the full expression of your life's purpose.

You may have to practice this more than once. Forgiveness is a process. You can incorporate this kind of activity into part of regular meditation practice. You have to be willing to be vulnerable to the feelings that will come up, and you have to be ready to accept that you did the things for which you are ashamed. You also have to be willing to look honestly at the context in which you behaved the way you did. When you acknowledge the feelings that led to your actions, you can build compassion for how you reacted. And then you can offer yourself forgiveness. Doing this regularly will reinforce not only the forgiveness you deserve but also the truth about your higher self. As part of this process, you also might feel the desire to ask forgiveness from someone you have harmed. This can be difficult, but it can also help you, and the person you harmed, to heal. If you choose to ask forgiveness, a good method is to a) simply state what you did without offering excuses and without self-blaming; b) express how you think your actions affected the other person without judgment or expressions of how they should have reacted; c) express how you intend to avoid making the same mistake in the future; and d) ask their forgiveness. The act of forgiving yourself or others helps you to heal and to free yourself from the constrictive self-judgments that keep you from realizing your true potential. It also allows you to accept yourself for who you are unconditionally.

Unconditional Self-Acceptance

When we are self-accepting, we are able to accept all parts of ourselves. We can accept the shadowy parts and learn to love them as much as we love the parts we like. In fact, for unconditional self-acceptance, we must do this. We learn self-acceptance from our parents. As children, we are only able to accept ourselves to the degree our parents accept us, and thus, if we faced adverse judgment from our parents, we generally will treat ourselves the same way they did. But, we can learn how to be different with ourselves. The key to doing this is developing self-compassion. Part of developing that compassion is to realize that you have been trained from an early age to prove your worth to others. This starts with your parents, but it spreads to teachers, friends, and others in your life. These approval-seeking behaviors are the legacy of our parents' conditional love. When we examine the scars we have from these early childhood experiences, we almost always increase our self-compassion. We come to understand that we are all part of the walking wounded; everyone has some scars to bear. As we recognize our common humanity, we are better able to provide ourselves with the kindness we have withheld for so long.

As we go through this heartfelt process, we can examine each area of self-rejection or denial, and we can bring into the light of understanding that our actions were part of our inability to develop better strategies--we were only children, after all. We can then begin to dissolve the exaggerated feelings of shame and guilt. We can realize that what was expected of us at that time was simply an unrealistic standard. It is from this space of self-compassion and common humanity that we can truly forgive ourselves and those who may have harmed us. And, it is in that space that we can unconditionally accept ourselves for who we are. We can embrace even the shadow parts of ourselves that result from our background and biology. We can integrate those shadows into our whole and use their gifts in more loving, caring ways. We can also view the challenges we faced as gifts that truly made us stronger. And, we can go forward with the knowledge that we are sure to make more mistakes, but we know the higher truth about ourselves. We know we are not our actions, and that we are continually changing and growing as part of the human experience. That is genuine, unconditional self-acceptance.

Self-Acceptance Quotes

Sometimes it helps to get inspiration from others who speak to our struggles. It helps us to understand that our struggles are a common human experience. Here are three quotes that speak to me personally:

"What if each time you experienced an emotion, you acknowledged it, accepted it, and became curious about its message for you (instead of trying to make it go away or make it last longer)? Imagine how this could change your life. Imagine how heard, loved, and honored you would feel if you really listened to yourself."

— Vironika Tugaleva

"Option A: Spend your life trying to get others to accept you. Option B: Accept yourself, and spend your life with others who recognize what a beauty you are."

— Scott Stabile

"No amount of self-improvement can make up for any lack of self-acceptance."

— Robert Holden

I hope you can take the same inspiration from these thoughts as I have. Use these wise words to motivate you as you make that sometimes difficult journey to unconditional self-acceptance.

Chapter Summary

In this chapter, we have examined the emotional states that disturb our inner peace, we discussed practical actions that you can take to restore your sense of inner peace, and we have examined the concept of self-acceptance.

We defined self-acceptance and discussed using intentionality to change how you think about yourself and your perceived flaws. We described how important self-compassion and self-forgiveness are to unconditional self-acceptance, and how adopting these ways of interacting with ourselves can free us from restrictive self-judgments. We described exercises you can use to establish unconditional self-acceptance through self-forgiveness.

In the next chapter, we'll examine self-awareness. We'll look at the origins of self-awareness, why we often lack self-awareness, how to regain it, and how to create a daily habit of self-reflection.

Chapter Five:
Self-Awareness

Before we begin discussing the origins of self-awareness, we should define what we're talking about. The kind of self-awareness we're discussing here is defined as having a clear understanding of your personality, including both your strengths and weaknesses as well as your thoughts, beliefs, emotions, and motivations. Being acutely self-aware means, in short, you know yourself, and you understand your motivations. It often requires taking a "deep dive" into what has shaped you and how that interacts with your emotions and thoughts to guide your behavior. It also means checking in with yourself at any moment to understand how events are impacting your emotional state. And, self-awareness is the foundation for emotional intelligence as well as self-leadership and mature adulthood. But where does this come from, and how do we develop it?

The Origin of Self-Awareness

Understanding self-awareness means understanding a little bit about the brain. There are three basic systems in the brain: the neocortex, which is our conscious mind where most of our thoughts happen; the limbic system, which is the subconscious "heart-centered" area where our emotions arise; and the basal ganglia, which is the unconscious "gut-centered" area where our instincts are activated. All three areas are involved in cultivating self-awareness. The neocortex is our conscious mind that we can access at any time. The limbic system is our subconscious mind, where we store emotions, value judgments, and memories. Lastly, the basal ganglia uses the information it receives from our gut to generate an unconscious instinctual response. It does so without checking with the other two regions of the brain (Cascio 2015; Strecher 2015). You can begin to see how all of these regions can affect our feelings and our experience at any moment in time.

As we go through life accumulating experiences, we react to those experiences using all three systems. We respond with our conscious neocortex--that is, we think about and rationalize the experience--and we use the subconscious limbic system to generate and store emotions we have around the experience, and those emotions generate a gut feeling that goes through the basal ganglia to activate appropriate instinctual responses. So, for example, if you feel fear, you may be analyzing what to do, but your negative emotions are being recorded and stored, and your gut feeling is stimulating an instinctual fear response. Most of this is happening on a subconscious or unconscious level. To generate self-awareness, we want to consciously access all of these areas in order to fully understand what we think and feel, and how that guides our actions.

As with learning any new skill, cultivating self-awareness means passing through four stages (Jeffrey 2019):

> **1.** Unconscious incompetence--this is where you don't know how bad you are at something until you try. You don't know you can't play the piano until you play a few chords.

> **2.** Conscious incompetence--this is where you are now aware of the fact that you are not good at doing something. You now understand that you can't play the piano.

> **3.** Conscious competence--this is where you make a committed effort to learn a new skill, and because of your dedication and practice, you have now reached a level where you are reasonably good at this skill. You can play the piano.

But, to get to this stage, you have to be willing to work through some uncomfortable feelings that arise as a result of your conscious incompetence.

4. Unconscious competence--this is the brass ring. This is where you can now perform the skill effortlessly. You can sit down at the piano without sheet music and play songs easily. This is the stage where the magic happens.

Most people will give up when those uncomfortable feelings arise — as with any skill, developing self-awareness means passing through these stages.

Why We Lack Self-Awareness

As with any skill, cultivating self-awareness demands practice and dedication. It's uncomfortable to feel incompetent, and so, most people will give up at that stage of the process. And, many people fail to develop self-awareness because, although they try, they target only the conscious neocortex rather than all three systems. A conscious connection to all three systems is a must if we are to truly understand the root of our thoughts, feelings, and actions. If we increase our sensitivity to our emotions and instincts, we can more thoroughly explore our thoughts, beliefs, and biases, and it is only then that we can truly understand our behavior. Another problem in developing true self-awareness is that most people think they're self-aware, but very few are. According to a multi-year study by The Eurich Group, a group of psychologists who provide executive coaching and leadership development programs for businesses, only 10 to 15 percent of people actually exhibit the characteristics of self-awareness; this despite the fact that some 85 to 90 percent of people think they are self-aware (Eurich 2018). Real self-awareness means being able to identify your values, your goals, your flaws, and your motivations, all with an understanding of how your past has influenced your behavior. It means acting consciously in every area of your life, exploring emotions as they arise, digging to get at the reasons for your triggers, and acting with intentionality to not only preserve but grow your self-awareness. It means understanding your place in the universe and the impact your actions have on yourself and others. Developing this takes a lot of work, and many people have too much fear of those uncomfortable emotions and instinctive reactions that will undoubtedly happen along the way. That's why we lack self-awareness, but if you've come to the realization that you're among the 85 - 90 percent of those who have not developed their self-awareness, what can you do to cultivate it?

Gaining Self-Awareness Through Others

While there are many things that other people cannot do for you as you develop your self-awareness, one thing that they can do is help you understand some of your own strengths and weaknesses through effective feedback. Effective feedback does not mean criticism, but rather it is honest and kind, specific, not general, descriptive, not critical; and focused on helping you build your strengths rather than highlight your weaknesses. Having a life coach or even a trusted friend who can give you this kind of feedback can help you understand areas of your behavior that you might not even realize are affecting your life. It is often easier to see shortcomings in other people than it is to see them in yourself. This isn't necessarily because you're critical of other people, but because you can see the ways in which your good friends are limiting themselves or even sabotaging their own success, whereas they are too close to the situation. Likewise, you can be too close to your situation to understand how others see you. That's how others can help us to see things we might not be willing to look at without their help. Life coaches are people who are trained to help you with this kind of thing, but if you don't have one of those, you can ask a good friend to provide you with some effective feedback. You might try asking them to answer the following questions honestly:

1. What behaviors do you believe are limiting my potential?

2. How do you feel when you're talking to me?

3. What do you think I'm good at? What are some of my weaknesses?

4. If you had to describe me to someone, what would you say?

5. Is there anything you avoid saying to me because you're afraid of how I'll react?

These questions will prompt them to give you the kind of feedback you can use to see better the areas in your own life where you might want to make improvements. That can help as you move on to the next steps of mindfulness and daily self-reflection.

Creating a Daily Habit of Self-Reflection

One of the first things you need to be able to do in order to practice self-reflection is to learn how to find your center. You have to be able to quiet your mind and free yourself from distractions in order to be able to truly explore the roots or your behaviors, emotions, and thoughts. When you are centered, there is no tension, you're alert but calm, and you're in the present moment. To be able to achieve this, it's important to have a place to sit that is quiet and free from distractions. It's helpful to close your eyes, so you are not visually distracted, and to focus on your breathing. Most people have trouble with this part because it's difficult to keep your mind quiet. Your "monkey mind" starts chattering incessantly, jumping from thought to thought, just like the monkeys in the trees. The key to quieting the "monkey mind" lies not in judging yourself when those thoughts intrude, but rather in accepting them, noticing what they are, and letting them go. For example, as you start to quiet your mind, you might start thinking, "I've got to get that report done at work tomorrow." What should you do? As soon as you notice you've been distracted by a thought, just think to yourself, "Oh, that's planning--I'm planning right now what I've got to do tomorrow," and let it go--visualize it actually rising up into the distance like smoke. Then, come back to your breath. Notice how fast you're breathing, how deep or shallow your breath is, and feel it coming in through the nose, traveling to the lungs, and coming back out again. Feel the rise and fall of your chest and your belly--that's right, breath into your belly. The goal is to achieve an even, rhythmic, deep breathing pattern.

Once you've got your breath flowing as you want, put your awareness on your body. Get in touch with the observer inside of yourself. Who is it that is noticing your thoughts? Who is it that notices your emotions? Use the observer to feel the surface you're sitting on, feel the contact with every part of your body. Don't just notice the contact with your backside, but your legs, your feet, the backs of your lower legs, your back against the back of the chair, and your hands resting on your legs. What do your legs and pants feel like? What does the fabric of the chair feel like on your legs? Can you feel your feet inside your shoes or socks? What do you hear? Try to divide the sounds you're hearing; try to hear those sounds we often relegate to background noise. Can you tease the different sounds apart? What are they? Do you find some of them to be annoying? What kind of reaction do they provoke in your body? Get in touch with the sensations in your body. Is there any area of pain, and what does that pain feel like? Is it sharp or dull? Is it constant or intermittent? Does it change? Try to notice these sensations before reacting to anything. For example, if you feel a sneeze coming on, try to notice what that feels like before you give in to the actual sneeze itself. Does your nose tickle? Do you feel a sharp inhale? Do your eyebrows rise as your eyes close? Notice what happens in your body before reacting to it. Feel the moment, and notice the stillness. Let yourself be still in the silence, and feel your body relax. Now, let the observer inform you about yourself.

What are you feeling? Is there something your mind just can't let go of? Navigate through as many emotions as arise in this state of mindfulness. Don't judge; just use the observer to notice what comes up and how what comes up feels in your body. For example, "Oh, that is shame. I'm feeling ashamed. How does it feel? Where do I feel that in my body? I feel pain in my stomach, in my bowels, and pressure across my chest. I feel like I can't breathe fully. I feel like I have to breathe in little gulps of air. My face feels flushed, hot. Why am I feeling that shame? Oh, I remember, my parents always told me that was bad. I did that once when I was young, and they told me how disappointed they were in me. And I have never let that go. I've never forgiven myself or gotten over that. That's why I reacted the way I did today when my child did that. Now, I understand." This is how the observer can help you get at the deeper foundations behind your beliefs, emotions, and behaviors. This is what lies beneath your conscious thoughts; what comes from the limbic system and the basal ganglia. This is the kind of self-reflection you have to practice in order to cultivate true self-awareness. It can be difficult work, and it is at times, exhausting, but if you practice it daily, it will open you to a deeper understanding, compassion, and acceptance of yourself. And it will be worth it. You'll develop much deeper compassion for yourself and others, and you'll improve the relationship you have with yourself. You don't have to treat every emotion this way, but you'll know the ones that need your attention because they will create a strong physical reaction. You will feel that stomachache or the pressure across your chest. Those are signals that this is coming from a deeper place, a kind of core truth you've accepted about yourself. They'll also likely generate strong reactions. If you find yourself suddenly yelling at your partner, your child, or your coworker, that's a good indication you've been triggered. Likewise, if you find yourself yelling at yourself, something's up, and it's time to reflect on that.

This kind of mindfulness meditation should be practiced daily. It doesn't have to be for long, maybe only 15 minutes, but it is important to do this regularly. Just like with the affirmations, repetition is key. Another practice that is helpful is to keep a journal of your insights. Allow yourself to write anything you want. There are no judgments in this journal. Let your thoughts and insights flow. Sometimes you write something, and you don't realize the full impact of what you've written until you go back and read it the next day. And, you'll start to see your growth as your self-awareness skills develop. Practicing this mindfulness meditation and journaling will help you to really understand your life story and how the events that happened left their marks. These practices will also help you to develop new goals for your life. Mindfully meditating, practicing self-reflection, and documenting your insights and goals will help you improve at planning and prioritizing your needs. And, you'll gain more insight into the story of you, and just how you roll! This can then help you understand the things about yourself you'd like to change. That is the gift of self-awareness.

Chapter Summary

In this chapter, we've discussed self-awareness. We've defined it and discussed how to develop it. We've looked at the helpful practices of asking others to inform us about how they see us, and how to use mindfulness meditation and self-reflection to gain a deeper understanding of our thoughts, emotions, and behaviors.

We noted that the three areas of the brain involved in our behaviors and thoughts are the neocortex, where our conscious mind forms our thoughts, the limbic system, where our subconscious mind forms and stores our emotions and memories, and the basal ganglia, where our unconscious mind uses our gut feelings to stimulate instinctive physical reactions to our emotions. We've discussed that the path the self-awareness means we must form a more conscious connection with all three of these areas.

The next chapter will present more powerful, positive affirmations that you can use in your practice of mindfulness meditation and self-reflection.

Chapter Six:
Powerful Affirmations-Two

This chapter presents more powerful, positive affirmations that you can incorporate into your daily mindfulness practice and self-reflection meditation, and any time you're feeling challenged by your day. Remember that the key to using affirmations is repetition. You should repeat each affirmation three times before moving on to the next one, and in this way, you can significantly strengthen the neural pathways that will make the physical response faster with the use of less energy.

Let's start with a few affirmations to help you calm yourself and feel centered (Bmindful.com, 2019; Garman, 2019; Motivationping.com, 2019):

1. My mind is quiet and stress-free.

2. My body feels calm and light.

3. I am at peace with myself and the world around me.

4. Nothing stands in my way of feeling calm and at peace.

5. My life is beautiful and bright.

6. My breath is slow and relaxed.

7. Everything is well in this moment.

8. I am calm and relaxed right now.

9. My mind is at peace in this very moment.

10. I am surrounded by good and supportive people in my life.

11. Around me, there is an endless pool of peace, harmony, and calmness.

12. I am completely relaxed, calm, and safe in this moment.

13. Right now, everything works perfectly for my good.

14. All my worries and problems are melting away.

15. I am calm, peaceful, and centered.

16. Each day I am practicing to be more and more relaxed.

17. Being calm and relaxed is my priority now.

18. I choose to be relaxed in any situation.

Here are several affirmations for self-awareness practice (Bmindful.com, 2019; Garman, 2019; Motivationping.com, 2019):

1. All my senses are alive and aware.

2. All my senses are finely tuned into this moment.

3. All my senses are observant of my surroundings.

4. Because I am always mindful, I am never bored.

5. Every day I become more and more aware of how we are all connected.

6. Each day I become more aware of my talents and abilities.

7. Every day I become more aware of the world around me.

8. Every day I strive to expand my awareness and understanding.

9. New awareness comes into my life daily.

10. Here and now is where I focus my attention.

11. I am alert and attentive to what's happening around me.

12. I am alert and present in every moment.

13. I am alive and aware in the present now.

14. I am always focused on the moment.

15. I am always mindful of my environment.

16. I am conscious of every present moment in my life.

17. I am conscious and aware at all times.

18. I am consciously aware of what I am thinking, feeling, and believing.

19. I am ever aware of my here and now.

20. I am ever mindful of the people in my life.

21. I am focused and alive in this present moment.

22. I am focused on the present moment at all times.

23. I am forever aware of the words I say to myself and to others.

24. I am fully alive and present at all times.

25. I am fully awake and alert at all times.

26. All aspects of my being, both visible and invisible, are vibrant and alive.

27. All my thoughts exist because I allow them to exist.

28. All that I have experienced in my life has made me better today.

29. Being self-aware is one of the top priorities in my life, and I practice this feeling every day.

30. Each time I pause to look inward, I draw closer to who I really am.

Here are a few aspirational and inspirational affirmations for mindfulness practice (Bmindful.com, 2019; Garman, 2019; Motivationping.com, 2019):

1. Every challenge I face makes me stronger and wiser.

2. Every day I become more aware of my strengths.

3. Every day I discover more of what makes me exceptional.

4. Every day I discover new talents that I possess.

5. Every day I practice always to be my true self.

6. Every day I appreciate myself more.

7. Every day I understand myself better.

8. Every facet of my life suits me perfectly.

9. Every moment I spend in quiet stillness brings me closer to my true self.

10. Every moment of every day, I am becoming more and more responsible for my life.

11. I am the change I want to see in the world.

12. We accept the love we think we deserve.

13. It is never too late to be what you might have been.

14. I inspire people around me.

15. I always see the good in people.

16. Everything I can imagine is real.

17. Nothing is impossible.

18. Peace begins with truth.

19. Who controls the past controls the future. Who controls the present controls the past.

20. Do not go where the path may lead, go instead where there is no path and leave a trail.

21. I can be changed by what happens to me. But I refuse to be reduced by it.

22. Pain is inevitable. Suffering is optional.

23. I turn my wounds into wisdom.

24. I never fail unless I stop trying.

25. I am important.

26. I am smart.

27. I am kind.

28. I do not fear failure.

29. I am capable of amazing things.

30. Nothing can stop me from achieving my goals.

31. Happiness comes from my own actions.

32. I change the way I look at things, then the things I look at change.

Chapter Summary

In this chapter, we can see several positive, powerful affirmations related to calming your mind to center yourself. There are also numerous positive affirmations you can use as part of your daily self-reflection and mindfulness meditation practice. And, lastly, there are several inspirational affirmations that will help with your mindfulness practices. Remember that you should use these affirmations daily, and you should repeat each affirmation before moving on to the next one.

In the next chapter, you'll learn about self-worth. We'll look at the importance of self-worth, how to build it up, and the consequences of having low self-worth. We'll also examine what you should not use to determine your self-worth and how you can know your own value. We'll also discuss some practical ways to build your confidence.

Chapter Seven:
Self-Worth and Confidence

Before we begin to discuss how important self-worth and how to build it, let's define self-worth. The concept is certainly related to the concept of self-esteem, but there is a slight difference that psychology and life-coaching professionals make. Self-esteem, as we have seen, is what you think, value, and believe about yourself. Self-worth is the knowledge that you are greater than all of that; that what you are is loveable, necessary for this life, and of immeasurable value. Self-esteem is more about measuring yourself in accordance with external actions, whereas self-worth is about your inherent value as a human being. The difference between self-worth and self-confidence is similar; self-confidence pertains to your confidence about your abilities in specific areas, whereas self-worth is about your overall value as a person.

To highlight these differences, let's look at an example. Let's say you're a student who makes average grades, someone who does okay, but you're not going to be graduating *summa cum laude* (i.e., with straight As). Still, you know you will graduate. Your confidence in your ability to graduate relates to your ability to complete the tasks necessary to do so--that's your self-confidence. Now, let's say that you know and value the fact that you would never cheat to get better grades--that's your self-esteem. You value yourself as someone who would not cheat. But, above all of that, when you think of those straight-A students, you don't feel intimidated just because someone got better grades than you--you know that you are every bit as inherently valuable as they are and that you deserve happiness and love every bit as much as they do--that's your sense of self-worth. With these definitions in mind, we can now examine the value of self-worth and how you can build it up.

The Consequences of Low Self-Worth

As you can imagine, the consequences of low self-worth are serious. This can manifest in various ways. You can literally hate yourself, loathe your actions and thoughts. That inner critic will run wild in your mind, constantly bringing you down. Not surprisingly, that results in depression, anxiety, fear, and anger. And, it will make you turn to external forces to seek approval, something that can never serve you well. You'll turn into the most ingratiating of people pleasers as you look for any validation. This will make you overly sensitive to even the most gentle criticism. You'll set unrealistic goals of perfectionism, something which you'll never be able to achieve. You'll likely also hate your body because you'll only focus on what you think are imperfections. And, your sense of low self-worth will actually become the cause of most of your problems. Much of this stems from a misunderstanding of what you should and should not use as a measurement of self-worth. So, let's examine what you definitely should not use!

What Should Not Determine Your Self-Worth

As we have discussed, what you don't want to do is turn to external factors as a measurement of your worth. These include any of the following items:

- *Your to-do list*: Just because you complete a task doesn't mean you are more valuable as a human. The same is true if you don't complete a task--it doesn't lower your value as a person.

- *Your job:* You might have a great job, maybe even one that helps people, but that doesn't change your value as a person even one little bit. Neither the most humanitarian job or the most menial job changes your value. You have value because you exist, not because of what you do.

- *Your age or your appearance:* These will both change over your lifetime. Your age is just a number, and your appearance is not what is inside of you, it's not what gives you value.

- *Your performance:* Your performance at work, at school, at the gym, or anywhere else is not the source of your value. Your value as a person is not found in things you do; it is found in who you are. And, you are much more than a grade or a performance evaluation or a fitness test.

- *Your friends* Whether they are virtually present or physically present, your friends are not who you are; they are not the source of your value. They should support you and prop up your self-esteem and self-worth, but they aren't the source--you're the source.

- *Your bank account:* Nothing material you possess--not your money, your house, your car, or anything else you own--is the source of your value. Your value as a person is independent of anything material.

- *Anything that is not you:* You should not use anything other than your own self to determine your self-worth. You are the source of your own self-worth, and you should never allow anyone to tell you anything different.

The Importance of Self-Worth and How to Build It

Your sense of self-worth doesn't rely on a comparison with other people or external factors. It is the knowledge that you are inherently valuable, regardless of any ability or talent you have or don't have. And, this value holds regardless of which characteristics about yourself you find valuable and which you think are not good. If you go through life's ups and downs with that understanding, you will have a solid foundation upon which you can build a life full of happiness and inner peace. You will feel better, and you will be less likely to engage in self-destructive behaviors like substance abuse or eating disorders. Even at your lowest point, if you know your value, you will understand that nothing can keep you down for long. Difficulties will pass, the good times are fleeting, but your sense of your own worth will remain with you throughout your life. That's the value of self-worth. So, how do you build it up?

As with anything, it helps if we can start to build up our self-worth early in life. If you're a parent, the most important thing you can do for your children is to show them unconditional love, respect, and positive regard. That means that even when they do the most frustrating things that most kids do, you still let them know that you love them, you respect them, and you hold them in positive regard. If you demonstrate unconditional love and respect even when your kids get failing grades or break the rules, you are telling them that your love and respect for them is not dependent upon any achievement or behavior--you love them simply because they exist--and that gives them permission to feel the same way about themselves.

The other thing it's important to give to your child is the chance to succeed. Success will boost their sense of self-confidence, and quite simply, it will make them feel good about themselves. Experiencing success will also open the door for them to take healthy risks as they move forward in life. One caveat here is that these should genuinely be successes based on what the child has accomplished. A helping hand is okay, but it should be the child who does the work to succeed. This will help them to build a healthy sense of self-confidence, self-esteem, and self-worth. These examples illustrate how you can help a child achieve a good sense of their own inherent value, but what if you're an adult who never got that kind of support from your own parents? How can you build your self-worth later in life?

One thing you need to do as an adult is to stop comparing yourself to other people. Your self-worth is not based on your bank account, your job, your relationships, your weight, or anything else that is outside of yourself. You are much more than all of these external elements in your life. The other thing to look at is that inner critic we all carry around, that little voice that seems to delight in telling you how wrong or bad you are. This critic is shaped in your childhood and often reflects the messages you received from your parents and other important people who were around during your early development. You can, however, challenge the critic. You can start by pausing whenever you hear the critic cranking up with those negative thoughts. Ask yourself, "Is there any basis in fact to what the critic is saying, and is it something you need to know?" For example, your critic starts in with, "Man, you really blew that job interview. They are never going to hire you now." Maybe, you find yourself going over a part of your interview again and again. What do you do?

The first step in dealing with this inner criticism is to acknowledge that it's happening. If you're dwelling on it, that clearly indicates you're suffering. Now, ask yourself why? Why are you thinking of negative thoughts about your performance? Why are you reviewing them again and again in your mind? As mentioned earlier, take a gentle tone with yourself, acknowledge that frightened part of yourself, and ask why you are frightened. You usually will get some insight into more than simply your performance in a job interview or any other task you might be working on. You'll often find it gets back to a core belief you accepted about yourself a long time ago. You might think, for example, "I'm afraid I'm just not good enough." That's about much more than one moment in your life. Now, be comforting to yourself. How would you speak to a good friend who came to you and expressed this same fear? It's likely you would say something like, "Look, I don't know if you got this job or not, but I can tell you that you are good enough to have gotten it. Maybe they're looking for someone with different talents than what you have, but you have many talents, and if you didn't get this job, it only means there is something much better for you out there. You are good, talented, and worthy of happiness, and you will find it." Now, say that to yourself; be as kind to yourself as you would be to your good friend.

It is in this exercise that you can see that self-compassion is paramount. You should remember that we all make mistakes and have different gifts. To use this example, perhaps you did mess up the interview, but that does not mean you aren't enough, and it doesn't mean you aren't worthy of happiness and success. It means you messed up an interview--nothing more. You'll get 'em next time. If you worry that you'll mess up *every* interview, then as we discussed earlier, stop worrying and take action. For example, ask a friend or family member to help you practice your interview technique. Get them to ask you the questions that the interviewer asked you (the ones you thought you messed up), and practice until you are comfortable with your response to their questions. And then, let go of the worry and the suffering. Move on, and do so with the knowledge that the fact you messed up an interview doesn't touch the reality of who you are--you are so much more than that. And, every time that mean-girl critic starts whispering in your ear, remind her that you are worthy, valuable, and more than enough and that you deserve happiness!

Another thing that can help you build your sense of self-worth is to take part in activities that add meaning to your life. Maybe you can volunteer at the animal shelter or help teach kids to read at the library. This will help you to see that you have valuable contributions to make, and that can give a huge boost to your feeling of self-worth. When you're helping somebody else, you're definitely valuable, no matter how well you did or didn't do in a job interview. These kinds of activities boost your self-esteem, and that, in turn, boosts your sense of self-worth. Additionally, in considering what is valuable to you, make a commitment to act on principle. Make a concerted effort to understand what your principles are, and then, to ensure that your actions correspond with your words. When you act out of integrity, you leave less room for that inner critic to speak out against you.

As you can see in these exercises, part of increasing your sense of self-worth is to increase your understanding of yourself. You have to think about what your values are in order to act with integrity. Understanding who you are is key to understanding how valuable you are. It's worth the time to engage in a relatively simple experiment:

1.   Imagine you had everything taken away from you, and I mean everything--your possessions, your relationships, your job, everything! If it helps to think about situations where this can happen, just think about the many refugees around the world and throughout history. Many of them lost everything, and many of them had a lot before that happened. So, no matter what you have, think about what would happen if you lost it all. What if all you had left was just you? How would that make you feel? What would you still have that would be of value? What's inside you that you would use to move forward with your life?

2. Now, think about the value you have that remains with you outside of those external factors. Can you understand that what you have inside of yourself is something that no one can take away from you? Your internal self stays, no matter what.

3. Now, explore this idea more deeply. Ask yourself, who am I? Answer by saying, "I am…" and by saying, "I am not…" Also, ask yourself, how am I? How am I in the world? How do other people see me and speak about me? What key life experiences or moments define who I am today? What brings me passion, fulfillment, and joy? What do I hold in high regard?

4. Once you have a good grasp of who you are, you can now look at areas where you struggle. Try asking yourself, "Where do I need to improve? What fears hold me back? What emotions hurt me on a regular basis? Where do I tend to let myself down consistently?"

5. Lastly, now look at where you shine. What abilities do you have? What are you really good at?

This exercise will help to boost your self-acceptance. You can see and accept what is inside of you, whether good, bad, or ugly. And, you can see the gifts you have received from your experiences in life. You can, in short, come to accept yourself unconditionally. That will help you enhance your self-love. And, that will increase your sense of self-worth. You know your self-worth is high if you no longer need to please other people, you know that you alone control how you feel about yourself, you know you have the power to respond to external events using your internal sources and resourcefulness, and you understand that your value comes from inside and that is a measure you set for yourself. All of this will allow you to take responsibility for yourself, and that gives you the power--not the external people or circumstances--in your life. This can be challenging work, but if you don't work at increasing your self-worth, there can be severe consequences.

Here's How You Know Your Value and Your Self-Worth

Here are the signs that you know your own self-worth:

> 1. You have positive self-esteem. This means you know and like yourself. You're comfortable with who you are, and you don't need the approval of people outside yourself.

2. You recognize your contributions and the difference they make. You have confidence in your own abilities to handle the situations that arise in your life. You're also not afraid to seek help when you need it, because you know that doesn't detract from your abilities.

3. You see yourself as a peer. You feel equal to the people around you. You know that their talents do not detract from yours and vice versa.

4. You know the value of your services. You don't undercharge for what you do, because you know that what you bring to the table is valuable.

5. You know your values. You have explored what you believe and committed to act with integrity. You know yourself.

6. You know that, no matter what, you're worthy of love. Your value is not dependent upon the mistakes you make any more than it's dependent on your successes.

7. You know that your value does not depend on material things. The car you drive, the house you own--these are things. They are not you.

8. You're not afraid to be alone. This is because you like yourself. You know you are good company.

9. You have compassion for yourself and others. You can see yourself in others because you are compassionate and can understand their situation.

10. You are grateful for your life. You realize that what you have received in your life as made you into the strong, valuable person you are.

When you do the work that will make these statements a reality for you, then you will know that you have a healthy concept of self-worth. Let's look at some practical ways to build your confidence.

Practical Ways to Build Confidence

Self-confidence, like self-esteem, is a key part of your self-worth. But what can you do to build up your confidence? Let's discuss a few ways you can do this. One of the first things that can help is if you can get things done. When you accomplish something, you gain the confidence that you can do things, and you can build on that. The best way to do this is to start with small goals and don't get ahead of yourself. Layout what you have to do one day at a time. If you have a big task to get done, take it one step at a time. How do you eat an elephant? One bite at a time. The same goes for that big task. Break it up into a series of small goals, and it will be easier to get done. Also, monitor your progress to make sure you're getting those smaller accomplished within the time frame you've set for the larger goal.

Another way to build your confidence is to make sure that what you do aligns with your values. If you believe in what you're doing, it's easier to do. For this, you have to know your values, and for that, you can use the exercises described earlier in this chapter. This is part of another step you can take--take care of yourself. This means exercise and try to eat right. Exercise releases endorphins in the brain that make you feel better. Exercise will also make you feel stronger, and that makes you feel confident.

Next, don't be afraid. It isn't failure that keeps you from succeeding in life; it's the fear of failure that cripples you. When you're afraid, you don't act confidently, and you often make more mistakes. If you know your values and what you're doing aligns with your values, then make a plan and move ahead with that plan without fear. If something comes up, adjust the plan, but don't let the fear take you over. Also, don't be afraid to stand up for yourself. Don't let other people push you to go against your values. Set boundaries with respect to what you will do, how fast you will do it, and who you listen to for advice. Keep the people that tear you down out of your life. That will significantly boost your confidence.

Along these lines, follow through with your actions and promises. If you say you will do something, do it. Keep your word. And, when you set a goal, make sure you're thinking long-term. Don't just go for short-term satisfaction; make sure your actions will be good in the long-term. Furthermore, make sure what you're doing is something that makes you happy. Even something unpleasant for you to do can ultimately make you happy. For example, you might not like cleaning your house, but it should make you happy that you're providing a clean environment for yourself and your family. That's thinking in the long-term and doing something that ultimately gives you pleasure. And, finally, don't worry about what other people think. Do what aligns with your values, makes you happy, and helps you build your confidence. The ultimate goal is building your self-worth, and nobody else can do that for you.

Chapter Summary

In this chapter, we have discussed the concept of self-worth. We have defined the term as the inherent value you have for yourself. It differs from self-esteem and self-confidence in that it is not related to the things you do in your life or the things you value about yourself. It is the worth you believe you have regardless of your accomplishments or your failures.

We also looked at different ways to raise your self-worth as well as your confidence. We described several exercises and explained what you should not use to determine your self-worth. Finally, we looked at how your confidence plays into your concept of self-worth and examined some practical ways to boost your confidence.

In the next chapter, we will discuss the concept of self-love. We will examine what it means, what is false self-love, what is true self-love, and ways you can cultivate self-love.

Chapter Eight: Self-Love

What Does Self-Love Really Mean?

We've talked about self-esteem, self-confidence, self-acceptance, self-worth, and now we're talking about self-love. But what does that mean? It's not, as some people mistakenly believe, something like narcissism. It's not about arrogance. It means having a high regard for your own well-being and happiness. And, that means taking care of yourself, accepting your weaknesses as something that makes you who you are, and having compassion for yourself. It means that you don't nitpick and criticize yourself, you give yourself space to grow, and you treat yourself with kindness. Everything we've been discussing to this point is all leading to helping you establish a true sense of self-love. But how can you know?

False Self-Love

Many people experience a sense of false self-love. How do you know it's false? Well, one way is if it is temporary. If you like yourself today because you lost five pounds, but that feeling goes away when you gain back two of those pounds, that's false self-love. What about if you're in a bad mood and you snap at someone in your life, do you still love yourself? If the answer is no, that's false self-love. If you've made your love for yourself in any way conditional, that's false self-love. So, what does true self-love look like?

True Self-Love

True self-love, like true love, is enduring. No matter what you do, if you truly love yourself, your love will remain constant. You might make mistakes, you might react negatively to other people in your life, you might even act against your own values, and you might feel you need to change, but true self-love remains constant through it all. True self-love understands your true self-worth. It means you understand your inherent value as a person, and you love yourself unconditionally because you know your value. If you really love yourself, you treat yourself like your best friend. You love everything about you. You set appropriate boundaries in your life so that you can get the rest that you need and practice copious amounts of self-care. True self-love is when you treat yourself like you would treat your very best friend in times of distress. You're kind to yourself, you're compassionate with yourself, you're gentle with yourself, and you do the things in your life that you need to do to take care of your health. That is self-love. How can you get you some of that? Let's take a look.

Ways to Cultivate Self-Love

Well, number one on the list is to start talking to yourself in a positive, powerful way by using the affirmations we've been discussing. And we'll present some more you can use in the next chapter. This will help you to be aware of and take control of your inner voice. It's vital to improving your self-esteem, your self-confidence, your self-worth, and your self-love. You want to eliminate the negative chatter in your head, and likewise, you want to eliminate the negative chatter of people in your life. If they're not building you up, they're not your friends. Who you allow in your life is an important way that you take care of yourself. Don't allow people who tear you down to get close to you. Pick the people who build you up instead. And, seek their counsel. They will give you kind, compassionate feedback.

We've seen this one before--stop comparing yourself. You'll notice that many of the ways you can build up your self-love are things we've talked about before in earlier chapters. That's because these things work on many levels. They can help build your self-esteem and self-love. These suggestions all work toward the same goal, and one area of your concept of self relates to another.

People who love themselves have high self-esteem, are confident in themselves, and they value themselves. And so, these suggestions help with each and every one of these concepts. If you compare yourself with other people, you will feel more negatively about yourself. That will lower your self-esteem, your self-confidence, your self-worth, and your self-love. Let me say it again--the gifts that other people have are not relevant to the gifts that you have. Their gifts neither add nor detract from yours. Let go of the comparisons.

Another thing you can do is to practice mindfulness and act with intentionality. Think about what you feel as your feelings arise, and how that relates to your concept of self. Think intentionally about how you will act on those feelings. Explore your feelings while practicing self-compassion--don't judge yourself for negative feelings, understand them. Toward this end, take time each day to quiet your mind and experience the stillness and peace of meditation. Along with this, take good care of yourself physically. Carve out time for exercise and try to eat healthy foods. This isn't related to how much you weigh, but it's about staying healthy. Feed your body, feed your mind, and feed your self-love. To do some of this, you might have to set boundaries. Let the people in your life know that it's important to take time for yourself. Also, let them know that you won't tolerate disrespectful treatment. You're open to constructive criticism, but you know your value, and you expect to be treated with respect. Even as you do this, realize you don't control other people. But, you do control yourself, and you have the right to remove yourself from their company if they are tearing you down.

An important step in building self-love is to forgive yourself. If you're practicing mindfulness meditation as discussed earlier, you can build self-compassion and learn how to forgive yourself. This is critical because it frees you to realize your full potential--which includes self-love--and it also allows you to forgive others. And, along with this, remember to be grateful for the life you have, including the challenges that have left you with the gifts that enabled you to survive to become the person you are today. As you practice mindfulness meditation and explore more about yourself and your feelings, it's also helpful to keep a journal. This can allow you to see things you might not otherwise see as you go along; that includes powerful insights and the progress you're making.

And finally, take the time to have fun in your life. Play like you did when you were that little kid, desperately waiting for recess. Experience the joy in just letting go and being--remember laying on your back and watching the clouds go by? Do that. Do you remember a time when you didn't let life weigh so heavy on your shoulders? You laughed, you made funny faces, you skipped through life. Taking time to do that again can help you love your life, and loving your life can help you love yourself.

Chapter Summary

In this chapter, we have discussed the concept of self-love. We defined what it is and what it is not. And, we examined a series of practical ways you can cultivate self-love. We discussed taking care of yourself, both mentally and physically, bringing positive, kind people into your life, being mindful and acting with intentionality, and letting go once in a while. We've also discussed how the other concepts of self--self-esteem, self-confidence, self-acceptance, self-compassion, and self-worth--are related to self-love. They are all part of an integrated whole.

In the next chapter, you will see many more examples of positive, powerful affirmations that are related to the concepts of self-worth and self-love.

Chapter Nine: Powerful Affirmations-- Three

As you have seen in Chapters 3 and 6, this chapter will present a series of positive, powerful affirmations related to the concepts we've been discussing. As before, repetition is key. You should practice saying a series of affirmations 3 - 5 times daily, and you should be sure to repeat each affirmation three times before moving on to the next one.

Here are 58 affirmations related to self-worth and self-love (Motivationping.com, 2019b):

1. I am worthy of love.

2. I am a good person and deserve to be loved.

3. I deserve to be loved and be treated with respect.

4. Being loved is my birthright.

5. Attracting love begins with self-love.

6. I radiate love to all beings.

7. I am full of unconditional love.

8. I am surrounded by people who love me unconditionally.

9. I am grateful for the people who love me unconditionally.

10. To love unconditionally is the greatest gift.

11. Today, I choose me.

12. I am worthy of infinite compassion.

13. I feel profound empathy and love for others.

14. I choose to stop apologizing for being me.

15. I am at peace with all that has happened in my life.

16. My life is filled with joy and abundance.

17. Happiness flows from me.

18. I feel pride in myself.

19. I am not the sum of my mistakes.

20. I have everything I need.

21. I feel beautiful, and I am beautiful.

22. I am empowered to create change in my life.

23. I focus on the bright side.

24. I am blessed.

25. I follow my own expectations, not the expectations of others.

26. I am in control of my own actions.

27. I overflow with creativity and good ideas.

28. I do not judge myself or others.

29. I did not get up today to "just" be average. I will excel.

30. I am not my negative thoughts or emotions.

31. Self-love comes to me with ease.

32. I embrace my flaws, knowing no one is perfect.

33. I have a caring heart.

34. I have all I need to live a happy life.

35. My struggles are just opportunities to learn.

36. My individuality is important.

37. I will be assertive when I need to be.

38. I am becoming the person I want to be.

39. I have the tools I need to achieve my dreams.

40. When I practice self-love, I become more lovable.

41. I deserve good things.

42. I control my fears; they do not control me.

43. I love the person that I am.

44. I am whole when I am alone.

45. I respect myself.

46. I have worth and inner beauty.

47. I will care for myself as much as I care for others.

48. I am willing to keep going when things get tough to achieve the success I deserve

49. My body is beautiful and expresses my spirit.

50. I am grounded, peaceful, and centered.

51. I respect my limitations and thank myself for the things I am able to accomplish.

52. My life is full of happiness and love.

53. I have the power to change my world.

54. I have much to celebrate about myself and my life.

55. I say no with ease.

56. I am more than a body.

57. I am growing and learning each and every day.

58. I lovingly embrace all my fears.

Chapter Summary

This chapter has presented 58 powerful, positive affirmations related to self-love and self-worth. Take the time to repeat a series of these affirmations several times each day, and anytime you feel you need a boost.

Final Words

Throughout this book, we have examined the concepts of self-esteem, self-confidence, self-acceptance, self-worth, and self-love. We have defined each and discussed the differences between them. We have also looked at the use of powerful, positive affirmations in your daily life to build up each of these important concepts. The consequences of a lack of self-love and all of the concepts of self we have discussed include, among other things, crippling depression, constant anxiety and fear, a growing sense of anger, and profound sadness. The benefits of improving each of these concepts of self include the fact that you will do better in your job or in school, you will be more confident in your actions, you will define and maintain healthy boundaries, you will take better care of your health, and quite simply, you will live longer (Moore 2019). You will love yourself, and because of that, you will take the kind actions you need to take in order to care for yourself, just as you would a dear friend or beloved family member. And, the science confirms that the benefits you will realize from building up these concepts of self are real.

Simply put, you don't have to live with the kinds of depression, anxiety, and anger that stifle your true potential. And, the truth is also that you don't deserve to live with those kinds of self-destructive emotions. To shine the light of understanding into the darkness found in your own mind means that you will free yourself to realize your life's purpose and achieve your true potential. You have taken the first step--you are learning about how to change the relationship you have with yourself. If you follow the recommendations we have discussed in this book--and engage in the exercises described, including the daily use of powerful, positive affirmations--you will improve the relationship you have with you. You will grow your self-esteem, your self-confidence, and your self-acceptance. And, when you build these up, you will also come to understand your true value and the fact that you are lovable. Life only gets better from there.

Make no mistake about it; many difficult emotions will arise throughout this process. But, if you use the loving techniques of self-care and treat those emotions with a true desire to understand them, you will come to see not only the value they had in shaping your life but how truly remarkable you are to have survived the conditions that generated those negative feelings.

You will see that you have done nothing wrong. Your actions made sense in the environment of surviving the challenges you faced. You did what you could with the strategies you had in that moment. But now, you have new strategies, and these are healthy mechanisms that allow you to face and overcome life's ups and downs. And, not only will you survive and overcome, you will thrive. You have the power in your own hands. You might not have received the unconditional love that every child deserves, but you can give that same unconditional love to yourself. And, in doing so, you will become the person you always knew you were. You will no longer need to compare yourself to anyone else. You will act with integrity, compassion, and kindness. You will treat not only others with the respect and kindness they deserve, but you will also treat yourself with that same respect, kindness, and love.

To do this, you will have to dive deep. You will have to practice mindfulness. You will have to be aware of your inner world, and how you are feeling in any given moment. And, you will have to explore those often very difficult emotions in order to understand their origins. You will also have to accept them and accept the shadowy parts of yourself that you haven't liked. They are part of you, and they have played a powerful role in your life. Bring them into the light of your self-love and treat them as that frightened inner child they truly represent by giving them--yourself--the compassion and understanding they so desperately need. In doing so, you will discover the gifts they bring to you. Once you have explored these hidden parts of yourself, you can begin to change your relationship to them--and that means to yourself. You can act with intentionality to be that calmer, happier person you deserve to be. You can bathe in the sweet, warm waters of true inner peace.

Through daily self-reflection, you can better understand your triggers, and when you are confronted with them, you will have new tools to use to dispel negative thoughts, emotions, and actions even before they happen. You will talk to yourself with the kindness, compassion, and love you deserve to have in your life. You will achieve the self-acceptance that brings with it the gifts of self-esteem and self-confidence. Once you accept yourself, you will find you can finally forgive yourself. And, once you have done that, you will find you can forgive those who have harmed you too. That is a gift you give yourself more than you give to them, but by showing them the light of your love, you give them permission also to forgive themselves. In short, you make the world a better place. You spread the light of self-love.

There is nothing more important you will ever do in your life. Welcome to this new beginning.

Bonus Powerful Affirmations

1. I deserve to be successful and live a happy life.
2. I have the power I need to change my low self-esteem.
3. I can forgive others and seek to understand their motives.
4. I have the power to make my own decisions and choices.
5. I am free to live my dreams and prioritize my desires.
6. I can choose positive thinking and happiness whenever I wish.
7. I am able and willing to change in all aspects of my life.
8. I act with confidence in having a general plan, and I am willing to accept and adapt to alternate outcomes.
9. It is enough to bring my best in anything I do.
10. I deserving of love and affirmation
11. I love meeting new faces and approach them boldly with confidence and enthusiasm.
12. I am creative and purposeful in whatever

I do.

13.   I love to grow and change while I adjust myself in new situations.

14.   I see only the good in others.

15.   I attract positive people into my life.

16.   I am unique and distinctive.

17.   I feel great about life and being myself.

18.   My life is rewarding and fun.

19.   Powerful opportunities exist for me in every aspect of my life.

20.   I love a good challenge because it will bring out the best in me.

21.   I choose to fuel my life with the power of my choices.

22.   I choose to be hopeful and happy. My life is truly wonderful.

23.   I choose to be grateful for all the good things I have in life. I live joyfully.

24.   I choose to be positive. I believe things will always work out for my own good.

25.   I possess great courage. I am willing to take action regardless of any fearful thought.

26.   Meeting new people comes easy to me. I create positive and strong relationships.

27.   I'm powerful in everything I create. I develop the life I desire.

28.   I love and accept myself who I am and who I want to become.

29. I trust in myself. My confidence starts with me.
30. I am successful.
31. I am passionate, and I inspire others with my life.
32. I am calm and at peace.
33. I contain unlimited power.
34. I believe things will always work out for the best.
35. I am loving and kind.
36. I am compassionate and care for others truly.
37. I will never quit.
38. I am persistent and focused.
39. Confidence is my second nature.
40. I am enthusiastic and energetic.
41. I treat everybody with respect and kindness.
42. I am flexible. I am able to change and adapt.
43. I have integrity. I am reliable. I do what I say I'll do.
44. I am smart and able.
45. I believe in myself.
46. I have many great qualities. I will recognize them.
47. I see the best in everyone.
48. I surround myself with people who bring out the best in me.

49. Today I let go of negative feelings and thoughts I've had about myself.
50. I love who I have become.
51. I will always grow and develop.
52. My opinions resonate with the person I am.
53. In everything I say and do, I am congruent.
54. I deserve success and happiness.
55. I hold the power to change myself.
56. I hold the power to change my circumstances
57. I forgive others and seek to understand their motives.
58. I make my own decisions and choices.
59. I am free to live my dreams and give priority to my desires.
60. I can choose to be happy no matter what my circumstances may be.
61. I am a great person. I respect myself deeply.
62. My opinions and thoughts are valuable.
63. I am confident. I can achieve anything.
64. I have so much good to offer this world.
65. Others admire and respect the person I am.
66. I am a wonderful person. I feel great about myself and my life.
67. I am worthy to carry high self-esteem.

68. I see and believe in my full potential.
69. I know I can achieve anything.
70. Feeling good about myself comes naturally.
71. Improving my self-awareness is important to me.
72. Speaking my mind in confidence is something I naturally do.
73. I notice I am more self-disciplined every day.
74. I enjoy practicing self-discipline.
75. I always do my best with the experience and knowledge I have and learn.
76. It is okay to make mistakes. They are opportunities to grow.
77. I always keep my promises.
78. I see myself in a positive light.
79. I love myself more every day.
80. I am willing to change.
81. I approve of who I am.
82. I care about who I am.
83. I give honor and respect to others.
84. I deserve good in my life.
85. I am more than enough.

Bonus Two: Complete Collection of 320 Powerful Affirmations Rearranged

1. I love the person that I am.
2. I overflow with creativity and good ideas.
3. All my senses are finely tuned into this moment.
4. I give praise freely.
5. I am courageous. I am willing to act.
6. I will never quit.
7. Everything is well in this moment.
8. All my senses are alive and aware.
9. I am more than enough.
10. I feel profound empathy and love for others.
11. I am a wonderful human being.
12. Every day I discover more of what makes me exceptional.
13. I know I can achieve anything.
14. I have many great qualities. I will recognize them.
15. I love and accept myself who I am and who I want to become.
16. I am worthy of all the good things that happen in my life.
17. All aspects of my being, both visible and invisible, are vibrant and alive.
18. I am more than a body.
19. Every day I become more aware of my

strengths

20. I know I can achieve anything.
21. I am surrounded by people who love me unconditionally.
22. Each time I pause to look inward, I draw closer to who I really am.
23. I change the way I look at things, then the things I look at change.
24. Because I am always mindful, I am never bored.
25. Life is fun and rewarding.
26. I live with joy and abundance.
27. I deserve to feel good about myself.
28. My life is filled with joy and abundance.
29. I give priority to my desires.
30. All that I have experienced in my life has made me better today.
31. I am willing to keep going when things get tough to achieve the success I deserve
32. I rejoice in the love I receive.
33. My body feels calm and light.
34. I am flexible and adapt to challenges and experiences.
35. I turn my wounds into wisdom.
36. I will be assertive when I need to be.
37. My mind is at peace in this very moment.
38. I love a good challenge because it will

bring out the best in me.

39. I am unique. I feel good about being alive and being me.
40. Each day I am becoming more self-confident.
41. I choose to be happy in every moment.
42. I am surrounded by good and supportive people in my life.
43. I am confident. I can achieve anything.
44. I am smart.
45. I deserve to be loved.
46. My opinions resonate with the person I am.
47. I choose happiness no matter what my circumstances are.
48. I see myself in a positive light.
49. I am confident that I can achieve anything.
50. I do not fear failure.
51. I am able and willing to change in all aspects of my life.
52. I never give up.
53. Happiness flows from me.
54. My body is beautiful and expresses my spirit.
55. I am alert and attentive to what's happening around me.
56. Every day I practice always to be my true self.

57. I am always mindful of my environment.
58. I deserving of love and affirmation
59. My life is beautiful and bright.
60. I always keep my promises.
61. I trust in myself. My confidence starts with me.
62. I am a great person. I respect myself deeply.
63. I am positive and optimistic.
64. I respect my limitations and thank myself for the things I am able to accomplish.
65. Do not go where the path may lead, go instead where there is no path and leave a trail.
66. Around me, there is an endless pool of peace, harmony, and calmness.
67. Every moment I spend in quiet stillness brings me closer to my true self.
68. My individuality is important.
69. I surround myself with people who bring out the best in me.
70. I respect myself deeply.
71. I will always grow and develop.
72. I am alert and present in every moment.
73. I am alive and aware in the present now.
74. It is enough to have done my best.
75. Today, I choose me.
76. I possess great courage. I am willing to

take action regardless of any fearful
thought.

77. I feel pride in myself.
78. I am calm, peaceful, and centered.
79. I deserve good in my life.
80. I have everything I need.
81. I always do my best with the experience
and knowledge I have and learn.
82. I have integrity. I am reliable. I do what I
say I'll do.
83. We accept the love we think we deserve.
84. I care about myself
85. I am enthusiastic and energetic.
86. Right now, everything works perfectly
for my good.
87. I make my own choices and decisions.
88. I love myself more every day.
89. Nothing stands in my way of feeling calm
and at peace.
90. I am capable of amazing things.
91. Self-love comes to me with ease.
92. I always expect the best and think
positively.
93. I have worth and inner beauty.
94. I am always growing and developing.
95. I say no with ease.
96. I can be changed by what happens to me,
but I refuse to be reduced by it.
97. Nothing can stop me from achieving my
goals.

98. I love who I have become.

99. I radiate love to all beings.

100. I am at peace with all that has happened in my life.

101. I appreciate the things I have.

102. Only I am responsible for making my choices and decisions.

103. I believe things always work out for the best.

104. I am worthy of love.

105. I am a wonderful person. I feel great about myself and my life.

106. It is okay to make mistakes. They are opportunities to grow.

107. Every challenge is a chance to grow.

108. I deserve the love I am given.

109. I am successful.

110. I am in full control of my life.

111. I am passionate, and I inspire others with my life.

112. I choose to be positive. I believe things will always work out for my own good.

113. Love supports me in expected and unexpected ways.

114. Happiness comes from my own actions.

115. I see and believe in my full potential.

116. Every challenge I face makes me stronger and wiser.

117. I respect myself.

118. Today I let go of negative feelings and thoughts I've had about myself.
119. I rejoice in my worth.
120. I treat everybody with respect and kindness.
121. Meeting new people comes easy to me. I create positive and strong relationships.
122. I am a good person and deserve to be loved.
123. I have the power to change myself.
124. I accept and love myself.
125. All my worries and problems are melting away.
126. Every day I become more aware of the world around me.
127. I have the power to change my world.
128. I choose happiness.
129. I am empowered to create change in my life.
130. I enjoy life to the fullest.
131. My breath is slow and relaxed.
132. I act with confidence.
133. I am respected by others.
134. I inspire people around me.
135. My growth is a continuous process. I am not stuck.
136. I can forgive others and seek to understand their motives.
137. I am smart and able.

138. It is enough to bring my best in anything I do.

139. In everything I say and do, I am congruent.

140. I am confident with my life plan and the way things are going.

141. It is never too late to be what you might have been.

142. I choose to be hopeful and happy. My life is truly wonderful.

143. My life is both beautiful and rewarding.

144. I appreciate everything I have. I live in joy.

145. I am loving and kind.

146. I am whole when I am alone.

147. When I practice self-love, I become more lovable.

148. I create the life I want.

149. Every day I understand myself better.

150. I have great ideas and always make meaningful contributions.

151. I am calm and relaxed right now.

152. I embrace my flaws, knowing no one is perfect.

153. I appreciate myself.

154. Others like and respect me.

155. I am consciously aware of what I am thinking, feeling, and believing.

156. I did not get up today to "just" be average. I will excel.

157. I am flexible and open to change in every aspect of my life.
158. I have the power I need to change my low self-esteem.
159. Nothing is impossible.
160. I am grateful for the people who love me unconditionally.
161. I forgive others and seek to understand their motives.
162. I have the power to make my own decisions and choices.
163. It's easy to make friends. I attract positive and kind people into my life.
164. I am driven.
165. I am grounded, peaceful, and centered.
166. I am persistent and focused.
167. I am flexible and open to new experiences.
168. I love who I am.
169. I am completely relaxed, calm, and safe in this moment.
170. All my thoughts exist because I allow them to exist.
171. My struggles are just opportunities to learn.
172. I am at peace with myself and the world around me.
173. I am focused on the present moment at all times.

174. I follow my own expectations, not the expectations of others.

175. Attracting love begins with self-love.

176. I trust myself.

177. I live present in every moment.

178. I choose to be grateful for all the good things I have in life. I live joyfully.

179. I am a great person.

180. I am a powerful creator.

181. New awareness comes into my life daily.

182. I attract positive people into my life.

183. I am strong. I live a powerful life.

184. I am in control of my own actions.

185. I choose to be happy right now. I love my life.

186. I deserve to be happy and successful.

187. I love to grow and change while I adjust myself in new situations.

188. I lovingly embrace all my fears.

189. I act with confidence in having a general plan, and I am willing to accept and adapt to alternate outcomes.

190. I have a caring heart.

191. I give honor and respect to others.

192. Speaking my mind in confidence is something I naturally do.

193. Being self-aware is one of the top priorities in my life, and I practice this feeling every day.

194. I care about who I am.
195. To love unconditionally is the greatest gift.
196. I approve of who I am.
197. I am compassionate and care for others truly.
198. Here and now is where I focus my attention.
199. Every moment of every day, I am becoming more and more responsible for my life.
200. My opinions and thoughts are valuable.
201. I am passionate.
202. I am forever aware of the words I say to myself and to others.
203. I have high self-esteem.
204. I am focused and alive in this present moment.
205. I'm powerful in everything I create. I develop the life I desire.
206. I always see the good in people.
207. I choose to fuel my life with the power of my choices.
208. My work gives me pleasure.
209. I deserve to be loved and be treated with respect.
210. I believe things will always work out for the best.
211. I make my own decisions and choices.

212. I approve of myself.

213. I choose to pursue my dreams and give priority to my desires.

214. I control my fears; they do not control me.

215. Being loved is my birthright.

216. I am successful right now.

217. I contain unlimited power.

218. My mind is quiet and stress-free.

219. I am not the sum of my mistakes.

220. Confidence is my second nature.

221. I have something special to offer the world.

222. I have the tools I need to achieve my dreams.

223. Others admire and respect the person I am.

224. I am not my negative thoughts or emotions.

225. I hold the power to change my circumstances

226. I have the power to change myself.

227. I am calm and peaceful.

228. I am enough.

229. I am ever mindful of the people in my life.

230. I am confident.

231. I am full of unconditional love.

232. I can choose to be happy no matter what

my circumstances may be.

233. I am unique. No one else can offer what I can to this world.

234. I am free to live my dreams and prioritize my desires.

235. I am blessed.

236. I believe in myself.

237. I deserve good things.

238. I can choose positive thinking and happiness whenever I wish.

239. I am conscious of every present moment in my life.

240. I notice I am more self-disciplined every day.

241. I choose to stop apologizing for being me.

242. My life is full of happiness and love.

243. I am conscious and aware at all times.

244. I see only the good in others.

245. I acknowledge my own self-worth.

246. I let go of the negative feelings about myself and accept all that is good.

247. I am at peace with myself.

248. I attract praise.

249. I easily forgive and understand others and their motives.

250. I have much to celebrate about myself and my life.

251. Everything I can imagine is real.

252. I deserve good in my life.
253. It's easy to meet people. I create positive and supportive relationships.
254. I am flexible. I am able to change and adapt.
255. I will care for myself as much as I care for others.
256. I never fail unless I stop trying.
257. I am worthy of infinite compassion.
258. I love meeting new faces and approach them boldly with confidence and enthusiasm.
259. Each day I am practicing to be more and more relaxed.
260. I love and respect myself.
261. I have all I need to live a happy life.
262. I love myself more each day.
263. I am fully alive and present at all times.
264. I am a unique and very special person.
265. Every facet of my life suits me perfectly.
266. I replace "I have to" with "I choose to."
267. I enjoy practicing self-discipline.
268. I see the best in everyone.
269. I am OK as I am.
270. Peace begins with truth.
271. Powerful opportunities exist for me in every aspect of my life.
272. Who controls the past controls the future. Who controls the present controls the past.

273. I am the change I want to see in the world.

274. Feeling good about myself comes naturally.

275. I have unlimited power at my disposal.

276. Amazing opportunities exist for me in every aspect of my life.

277. My thoughts and opinions are valuable.

278. I am worthy of having high self-esteem.

279. I feel beautiful. I am beautiful.

280. I am growing and learning each and every day.

281. I am worthy to carry high self-esteem.

282. All my senses are observant of my surroundings.

283. I am ever aware of my here and now.

284. Each day I become more aware of my talents and abilities.

285. I am free to live my dreams and give priority to my desires.

286. I am successful.

287. I am willing to change.

288. I have so much good to offer this world.

289. My opinions resonate with who I am.

290. I believe in my skills and abilities.

291. I focus on the bright side.

292. Every day I discover new talents that I possess.

293. I am becoming the person I want to be.

294. I am fully awake and alert at all times.
295. I feel great about life and being myself.
296. I receive all the useful information I need to succeed.
297. I love challenges; they bring out the best in me.
298. My life is rewarding and fun.
299. Every day I appreciate myself more.
300. Every day I strive to expand my awareness and understanding.
301. I am outrageously enthusiastic and inspire others.
302. I deserve to be successful and live a happy life.
303. I am important.
304. Pain is inevitable. Suffering is optional.
305. I deserve success and happiness.
306. I am unique and distinctive.
307. I stand by my decisions. They are sound and reasoned.
308. I choose to be relaxed in any situation.
309. Every day I become more and more aware of how we are all connected.
310. I breathe in confidence.
311. Being calm and relaxed is my priority now.
312. I am always focused on the moment.
313. I hold the power to change myself.
314. I am kind.

315. I believe in myself.

316. Improving my self-awareness is important to me.

317. I am creative and purposeful in whatever I do.

318. I have been blessed with health and happiness.

319. I am calm and at peace.

320. I do not judge myself or others.

Sources

Ackerman, C. (2019). *What is Self-Worth and How Do We Increase it? (Incl. 4 Worksheets)*. [online] PositivePsychology.com. Available at: https://positivepsychology.com/self-worth/ [Accessed 2 Oct. 2019].

Aham-adi, M. (2018). *50 Positive Affirmations for Self-esteem to Torpedo Your Confidence - THEZEROED*. [online] THEZEROED. Available at: https://thezeroed.com/positive-affirmations-for-self-esteem/ [Accessed 2 Oct. 2019].

Anon, (2019). [online] Available at: https://blog.mindvalley.com/positive-affirmations/ [Accessed 2 Oct. 2019].

Anon, (2019). [online] Available at: https://www.bestselfawareness.com/affirmations-for-success/ [Accessed 2 Oct. 2019].

Babcock, J. C., Jacobson, N. S., Gottman, J. M., & Yerington, T. P. (2000). Attachment, emotional regulation, and the function of marital violence: Differences between secure, preoccupied, and dismissing violent and nonviolent husbands. *Journal of Family Violence, 15*(4), 391-409.

http://dx.doi.org/10.1023/A:1007558330501

Blog, G. (2019). *Insecurity*. [online] GoodTherapy.org Therapy Blog. Available at: https://www.goodtherapy.org/blog/psychpedia/insecurity [Accessed 2 Oct. 2019].

Bmindful.com. (2019). *Self Awareness Affirmations - bmindful - the positive affirmation and self help community*. [online] Available at: http://bmindful.com/affirmations/self%20awareness [Accessed 2 Oct. 2019].

Brandt, A. (2019). *What Do We Mean By Self-Love - Dr. Andrea Brandt*. [online] Dr. Andrea Brandt, PhD, MFT. Available at: https://abrandtherapy.com/what-do-we-mean-when-we-say-self-love/ [Accessed 2 Oct. 2019].

Brave Belle. (2019). *What does "self-love" really mean and how to start loving yourself | Brave Belle*. [online] Available at: http://bravebelle.com/what-does-self-love-really-mean-and-how-to-start-loving-yourself/ [Accessed 2 Oct. 2019].

Bridges, F. (2019). *10 Ways To Build Confidence*. [online] Forbes.com. Available at: https://www.forbes.com/sites/francesbridges/2017/07/21/10-ways-to-build-confidence/#30ff534d3c59 [Accessed 2 Oct. 2019].

Camp, N. (2016). *100 Self Esteem Affirmations That Builds Self Worth*. [online] Committed To Myself. Available at: https://committedtomyself.com/100-self-esteem-affirmations-that-builds-self-worth/ [Accessed 2 Oct. 2019].

Cascio, C. N., O'donnell, M. B., Tinney, F. J., Lieberman, M. D., Taylor, S. E., Strecher, V. J., & Falk, E. B. (2015). Self-affirmation activates brain systems associated with self-related processing and reward and is reinforced by future orientation. *Social Cognitive and Affective Neuroscience, 11*(4), 621-629.

Cohen S, C.M. Alper, W.J. Doyle, J.J. Treanor, and R.B. Turner. (2006). Positive emotional style predicts resistance to illness after experimental exposure to rhinovirus or influenza a virus. *Psychosom Med.* 2006 Nov-Dec; 68(6):809-15.

Cohen, G. L., & Sherman, D. K. (2014). The psychology of change: Self-affirmation and social psychological intervention. *Annual Review of Psychology, 65*, 333-371.

Cresswell, J.D., J.M. Dutcher, W.M.P. Klein, P.T. Harris, and J.M. Levine (2013). Self-Affirmation Improves Problem-Solving under Stress. PLOS/One, https://doi.org/10.1371/journal.pone.0062593

Critcher, C. R., & Dunning, D. (2015). Self-affirmations provide a broader perspective on self-threat. *Personality and Social Psychology Bulletin, 41*(1), 3-18.

Develop Good Habits. (2019). *What Is Self-Awareness? (and 8 Ways to Become More Self Aware).* [online] Available at: https://www.developgoodhabits.com/what-is-self-awareness/ [Accessed 2 Oct. 2019].

Dunn, C. (2019). *10 Things You Can Do to Boost Self-Confidence.* [online] Entrepreneur. Available at:

https://www.entrepreneur.com/article/281874 [Accessed 2 Oct. 2019].

Ellsworth, B. (2019). *The Difference Between Self-Confidence and Self-Esteem - Step Into Success.* [online] Step Into Success. Available at: https://www.stepintosuccess.com/difference-self-confidence-self-esteem/ [Accessed 2 Oct. 2019].

Eurich, Tasha (2018). Insight: The surprising truth about how others see us, how we see ourselves, and why the answers matter more than we think. Currency: New York.

Falk, E. B., O'Donnell, M. B., Cascio, C. N., Tinney, F., Kang, Y., Lieberman, M. D., ... & Strecher, V. J. (2015). Self-affirmation alters the brain's response to health messages and subsequent behavior change. *Proceedings of the National Academy of Sciences, 112*(7), 1977-1982.

Garman, C. (2019). *Affirm Your Life: SELF-AWARENESS Affirmations.* [online] Affirmyourlife.blogspot.com. Available at: http://affirmyourlife.blogspot.com/2009/12/self-awareness-affirmations.html [Accessed 2 Oct. 2019].

George, B. (2019). *Know Thyself: How to Develop Self-Awareness.* [online] Psychology Today. Available at: https://www.psychologytoday.com/us/blog/what-is-your-true-north/201509/know-thyself-how-develop-self-awareness [Accessed 2 Oct. 2019].

Gold, A. (2019). Why Self-Esteem Is Important for Mental Health | NAMI: National Alliance on Mental Illness. [online] Nami.org. Available at:

https://www.nami.org/Blogs/NAMI-Blog/July-2016/Why-Self-Esteem-Is-Important-for-Mental-Health [Accessed 2 Oct. 2019].

Greenberg, M. (2019). *8 Powerful Steps to Self-Love.* [online] Psychology Today. Available at: https://www.psychologytoday.com/us/blog/the-mindful-self-express/201706/8-powerful-steps-self-love [Accessed 2 Oct. 2019].

Hays, J. (2019). *30 Ways To Practice Self-Love And Be Good To Yourself.* [online] Lifehack. Available at: https://www.lifehack.org/articles/communication/30-ways-practice-self-love-and-good-yourself.html [Accessed 2 Oct. 2019].

Healthysleep.med.harvard.edu. (2019). *Sleep and Disease Risk | Healthy Sleep.* [online] Available at: http://healthysleep.med.harvard.edu/healthy/matters/consequences/sleep-and-disease-risk [Accessed 11 Oct. 2019].

Ho, V. (2019). *The Differences Between Self-Esteem and Self-Confidence | The Up Lab.* [online] Theuplab.com. Available at: http://theuplab.com/2013/09/09/differences-self-esteem-confidence/ [Accessed 2 Oct. 2019].

Jeffrey, S. (2019). *15 Self Awareness Activities and Exercises to Build Emotional Intelligence.* [online] Scott Jeffrey. Available at: https://scottjeffrey.com/self-awareness-activities-exercises/#How_to_Gain_Self_Awareness_Through_Others [Accessed 2 Oct. 2019].

JourneyPure Emerald Coast. (2019). *Shredding self-doubts, finding personal growth within in addiction recovery*. [online] Available at: https://emeraldcoastjourneypure.com/addiction-recovery-self-doubt/ [Accessed 2 Oct. 2019].

Kan, S.K., A.D. Galinskey, L.J. Kray, and A. Shirako (2015). Power Affects Performance When the Pressure Is On: Evidence for Low-Power Threat and High-Power Lift. *Personality and Social Psychology Bulletin*, 41(5), 726-735.

Kay, K. (2019). *Confidence VS Self-Esteem - The Confidence Code*. [online] The Confidence Code. Available at: https://theconfidencecode.com/2014/03/confidence-vs-self-esteem/ [Accessed 2 Oct. 2019].

Khoshaba, D. (2019). *A Seven-Step Prescription for Self-Love*. [online] Psychology Today. Available at: https://www.psychologytoday.com/us/blog/get-hardy/201203/seven-step-prescription-self-love [Accessed 2 Oct. 2019].

Kloppers, M. (2019). *40 Ways to Achieve Peace Of Mind and Inner Calm*. [online] Lifehack. Available at: https://www.lifehack.org/articles/communication/40-ways-achieve-peace-mind-and-inner-calm.html [Accessed 2 Oct. 2019].

Lifehacker.com. (2019). [online] Available at: https://lifehacker.com/self-confidence-and-self-esteem-aren-t-the-same-thing-1737949859 [Accessed 2 Oct. 2019].

Live Bold and Bloom. (2019). *13 Steps To Inner Peace (Even In A Busy Stressful World)*. [online] Available at: https://liveboldandbloom.com/09/lifestyle/inner-peace [Accessed 2 Oct. 2019].

Love Your Mind. (2019). *How to find self-acceptance and live with intention — Love Your Mind*. [online] Available at: https://www.loveyourmindwpg.com/blog/self-acceptance-intention [Accessed 2 Oct. 2019].

Manson, M. (2019). *Why You Suck at Self-Awareness*. [online] Mark Manson. Available at: https://markmanson.net/self-awareness [Accessed 2 Oct. 2019].

Mindtools.com. (2019). *Using Affirmations: – Harnessing Positive Thinking*. [online] Available at: https://www.mindtools.com/pages/article/affirmatio ns.htm [Accessed 2 Oct. 2019].

Mindvalley Blog. (2019). *80 Powerful Affirmations That Could Change Your Life*. [online] Available at: https://blog.mindvalley.com/positive-affirmations/ [Accessed 13 Oct. 2019].

Moore, C. (2019). *Positive Daily Affirmations: Is There Science Behind It?*. [online] PositivePsychology.com. Available at: https://positivepsychology.com/daily-affirmations/ [Accessed 2 Oct. 2019].

Morin, A. (2019). *5 Things That Shouldn't Determine Your Self-Worth (But Probably Do)*. [online] Inc.com. Available at:

https://www.inc.com/amy-morin/how-do-you-measure-your-self-worth.html [Accessed 2 Oct. 2019].

Morin, A. (2019). *10 Things Mentally Strong People Give Up to Gain Inner Peace*. [online] Inc.com. Available at: https://www.inc.com/amy-morin/10-things-mentally-strong-people-give-up-to-gain-inner-peace.html [Accessed 2 Oct. 2019].

Motivationping.com. (2019). *Peace & Calming Affirmations That Work Fast*. [online] Available at: https://motivationping.com/peace-calming-affirmations/ [Accessed 2 Oct. 2019].

Motivationping.com. (2019b). *Self-Love & Self-Esteem Affirmations*. [online] Available at: https://motivationping.com/self-love-esteem-affirmations/ [Accessed 2 Oct. 2019].

News. (2019). *An active social life may help you live longer*. [online] Available at: https://www.hsph.harvard.edu/news/hsph-in-the-news/active-social-life-longevity/ [Accessed 11 Oct. 2019].

Owlcation. (2019). *Confidence & Self Esteem—What's the Difference?*. [online] Available at: https://owlcation.com/social-sciences/Whats-the-difference-between-self-esteem-and-confidence [Accessed 2 Oct. 2019].

Patterson, M. (2019). *Seven Signs You Know Your Value and Self-Worth | Management 3.0*. [online] Management 3.0. Available at: https://management30.com/blog/knowing-your-value-self-worth/ [Accessed 2 Oct. 2019].

Pennock, S. (2019). *19 Self-Acceptance Quotes For Relating To Yourself In A Healthier Way.* [online] PositivePsychology.com. Available at: https://positivepsychology.com/self-acceptance-quotes/ [Accessed 2 Oct. 2019].

Pillay, S. (2019). *Greater self-acceptance improves emotional well-being - Harvard Health Blog.* [online] Harvard Health Blog. Available at: https://www.health.harvard.edu/blog/greater-self-acceptance-improves-emotional-well-201605169546 [Accessed 2 Oct. 2019].

PsychAlive. (2019). *The Importance of Self-Worth - PsychAlive.* [online] Available at: https://www.psychalive.org/self-worth/ [Accessed 2 Oct. 2019].

PsychAlive. (2019). *How to Overcome Insecurity: Why Am I So Insecure?.* [online] Available at: https://www.psychalive.org/how-to-overcome-insecurity/ [Accessed 2 Oct. 2019].

Puff, R. (2019). *How to Find Inner Peace.* [online] Psychology Today. Available at: https://www.psychologytoday.com/us/blog/meditation-modern-life/201710/how-find-inner-peace [Accessed 2 Oct. 2019].

Raj, A. (2019). *Positive Affirmations for self esteem? 33 powerful affirmations to skyrocket your confidence.* [online] Medium. Available at: https://medium.com/@ayush.raj1806/positive-affirmations-for-self-esteem-33-powerful-affirmations-to-skyrocket-your-confidence-9423f000eda8 [Accessed 2 Oct. 2019].

Salzberg, S. (2019). *Practice Self-Compassion with Forgiveness - Mindful.* [online] Mindful. Available at: https://www.mindful.org/practice-self-compassion-with-forgiveness/ [Accessed 2 Oct. 2019].

ScienceDaily. (2019). *Praising children for their personal qualities may backfire.* [online] Available at: https://www.sciencedaily.com/releases/2013/02/130 227183316.htm [Accessed 11 Oct. 2019].

Seltzer, L. (2019). *The Path to Unconditional Self-Acceptance.* [online] Psychology Today. Available at: https://www.psychologytoday.com/us/blog/evolutio n-the-self/200809/the-path-unconditional-self-acceptance [Accessed 2 Oct. 2019].

Silva, C. (2017). *Social Media's Impact on Self-Esteem.* [online] Huffpost.com. Available at: https://www.huffpost.com/entry/social-medias-impact-on-self-esteem_b_58ade038e4b0d818c4f0a4e4?guccounter= 1 [Accessed 2 Oct. 2019].

Stanwyk, M. (2019). *The 10 Thought Habits of People with High Self-Worth.* [online] Whole Life Challenge. Available at: https://www.wholelifechallenge.com/the-10-thought-habits-of-people-with-high-self-worth/ [Accessed 2 Oct. 2019].

Travel Soul Therapy. (2019). *Compassionate Self-Forgiveness — Gateway To Transformation..* [online] Available at: http://www.travel-soul-therapy.com/compassionate_self-forgiveness.html [Accessed 2 Oct. 2019].

Watt, P. (2019). *These 8 Emotional Patterns Disturb Your Inner Peace.* [online] Tranquil Monkey. Available at: https://tranquilmonkey.com/these-8-emotional-patterns-disturb-your-inner-peace/ [Accessed 2 Oct. 2019].

Webber, B. (2019). *There's a Difference Between Confidence and Self-Esteem.* [online] Medium. Available at: https://medium.com/@BridgetWebber/theres-a-difference-between-confidence-and-self-esteem-d0781282ec11 [Accessed 2 Oct. 2019].

Wehrenberg, M. (2019). *When Self-Compassion Requires Self-Forgiveness.* [online] Psychology Today. Available at: https://www.psychologytoday.com/us/blog/depression-management-techniques/201405/when-self-compassion-requires-self-forgiveness [Accessed 2 Oct. 2019].

Western, D. (2019). *100 Spectacular Self-Love Quotes to Memorise.* [online] Wealthy Gorilla. Available at: https://wealthygorilla.com/100-best-self-love-quotes/ [Accessed 2 Oct. 2019].

WHO.int. (2019). *Depression.* [online] Available at: https://www.who.int/news-room/fact-sheets/detail/depression [Accessed 11 Oct. 2019].

Wong, S. (2019). *13 Things That Don't Determine Your Self-Worth.* [online] Shine. Available at: https://advice.shinetext.com/articles/12-things-that-dont-determine-your-self-worth/ [Accessed 2 Oct. 2019].

Yanek L.R., B.G. Kral, T.F. Moy, D, Vaidya, M. Lazo, L.C. Becker, and D.M. Becker. (2013). Effect of positive well-being on incidence of symptomatic coronary artery disease. *Am J Cardiol.* 2013 Oct 15;112(8):1120-5. doi: 10.1016/j.amjcard.2013.05.055.

Taking Charge of Your Health & Wellbeing. (2019). *How Do Thoughts and Emotions Affect Health? | Taking Charge of Your Health & Wellbeing.* [online] Available at: https://www.takingcharge.csh.umn.edu/how-do-thoughts-and-emotions-affect-health [Accessed 27 Sep. 2019].